Winning in the Opening

CADOGAN CHESS SERIES

Other titles for the improving player available from Cadogan include:

Chess Endings:
Essential Knowledge
Yuri Averbakh

Chess Middlegames:
Essential Knowledge
Yuri Averbakh

Chess for Tigers
Simon Webb

How Good is Your Chess?
Daniel King

Danger in Chess
Amatzia Avni

Improve Your Chess *Now*
Jonathan Tisdall

Creative Chess: Expanded Edition
Amatzia Avni

Basic Chess Openings
Gabor Kallai

How to Win at Chess
Daniel King

Mastering Chess
Chandler, Kopec, Morrison, Davies
and Mullen

Three Steps to Chess Mastery
Alexei Suetin

Garry Kasparov's Chess
Challenge
Garry Kasparov

For a complete catalogue of CADOGAN CHESS books
(which includes the Pergamon Chess and
Maxwell Macmillan Chess lists) please write to:
Cadogan Books plc, 27-29 Berwick Street, London W1V 3RF
Tel: (0171) 287 6555 Fax: (0171) 734 1733

Winning in the Opening

John Walker

CADOGAN
chess
LONDON, NEW YORK

First published 1997 by Cadogan Books plc, 27-29 Berwick St.,
London W1V 3RF

Distributed in North America by Simon & Schuster,
Paramount Publishing, 200 Old Tappan Road, Old Tappan,
New Jersey 07675, USA.

British Library Cataloguing in Publication Data
A CIP catalogue record for this book is available from the British
Library

ISBN 1 85744 200 8

Edited by Graham Burgess and typeset by Petra Nunn for
Gambit Publications Ltd, London

Printed in Great Britain by BPC Wheatons Ltd, Exeter

Contents

Notation

Throughout this book we use the long form of algebraic notation.

The Board

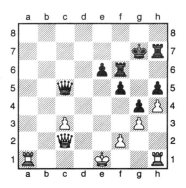

Notation Diagram

Each row of squares across the board is called a *rank*, and is given a number starting from White's side.

Each row of squares running up the board is called a *file*, and is given a letter starting from White's left hand side.

Each square is named by first giving the file letter and then the rank number. In our diagram a white rook stands at a1, the white queen at c2, the black king at g7, and so on.

The Symbols

We use symbols as abbreviations for pieces and chess terms.

♔	=	King	e.p.	=	*en passant*
♕	=	Queen	0-0	=	castles on the kingside
♖	=	Rook	0-0-0	=	castles on the queenside
♗	=	Bishop	x	=	takes
♘	=	Knight	-	=	moves to
The pawn has no symbol.			+	=	check

We use ! to show a good move and ? to show a bad move.

!? is used to show an interesting move, one which might actually be a mistake but which leads to complications and gives problems to the opponent.

?! is a move that is probably a bad idea, !! shows that a move is brilliant and very strong, while ?? is used for a terrible mistake.

Writing the Moves

There are four things to be written when writing a move.

a) The symbol for the piece which moves (unless it is a pawn).
b) The square it was standing on before moving.
c) The action it makes.
d) The square it moves to.

In the diagram on the previous page, the white rook which stands on a1 can move to a8 at the other end of the board. This would be written:
♖a1-a8

If check is given, the check sign is written after the move. In the diagram White can give check by moving his rook to a7:
♖a1-a7+

But then Black could capture the rook with his queen:
...♕c5xa7

As the pawn has no symbol the first of our four steps is left out when we write a pawn move. If White advances the pawn in front of his queen, the move is written:
c3-c4

Naming Pawns

A pawn is named after the file on which it stands. In the diagram, the pawn on c3 is White's c-pawn. The pawn on e6 is Black's e-pawn, and so on.

Naming Pieces

If in the commentary it is necessary to distinguish between two similar pieces of the same colour, each is named after the square it stands upon. In the diagram Black has two rooks, his f6-rook and his h7-rook.

Some chess terms and expressions

RANK: a row of squares running across the board from left to right. The row from a1 to h1 is White's first rank.

FILE: a row of squares running up the board from the white to the black side. The a-file runs from a1 to a8 and so on.

THE CENTRE: the middle of the board. In particular the squares e4, d4, e5 and d5.

KINGSIDE: the half of the board to White's right; the e-, f-, g- and h-files.

QUEENSIDE: the other half of the board: the a-, b-, c- and d-files.

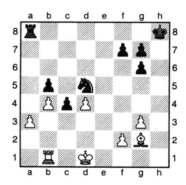

Terms Diagram

OPEN FILE: a file upon which neither side has a pawn. In the diagram the e-file and h-file are both open.

HALF-OPEN FILE: a file upon which only one player has a pawn. In the diagram Black has two half-open files, the a-file and the d-file, while the c-file is half-open for White.

BLUNDER: a mistake.

COMBINATION: a series of moves gaining an advantage.

DEVELOPMENT: bringing pieces into play in the opening.

DOUBLED PAWNS: two pawns of the same colour on the same file. In the diagram Black has doubled pawns on the g-file.

EN PRISE: a piece is said to be *en prise* when it is threatened with capture. In the diagram the black knight is *en prise* because it is not defended and it is attacked by the white bishop.

FIANCHETTO: a bishop developed to b2, g2, b7 or g7. In the diagram White's bishop on g2 is fianchettoed.

FLIGHT SQUARE: a square to which an attacked piece may run.

FORK: a double attack. If Black plays ...♘d5-c3+ he will be forking the white king and rook.

HOLE: a square in a player's position which cannot be defended by a pawn.

INITIATIVE: a player has the initiative when he begins to play forcefully and restrict his opponent's choice of replies.

ISOLATED PAWN: a pawn which has no pawn of the same colour on the files either side of it. In the diagram the white pawn on d4 is isolated because White does not have a pawn on the c- or e-file.

LOOSE: undefended.

MAJOR/MINOR PIECES: queens and rooks are the major pieces; bishops and knights are the minor pieces.

MATERIAL: a general term for pieces and pawns.

PIN: a piece is pinned when it cannot move without exposing a more valuable piece to capture. In the diagram, the white bishop pins Black's knight against his rook.

SACRIFICE: giving up material in the hope of gaining some kind of advantage.

THE EXCHANGE: the advantage of a rook against a knight or bishop. In the diagram after 1...♘d5-c7 2 ♗g2xa8 ♘c7xa8, Black has lost the exchange.

Introduction

Winning is nice ... it makes us feel good!

Winning in the opening is particularly pleasant. The game is over quickly and you can wander around the room with a self-satisfied smile upon your face whilst your team-mates are still struggling with their own games. Then when they have finished, you have a lovely short game-score to show to them to demonstrate your brilliance! However...

Warning!

You must not expect to win a game in the opening!

All games of chess, even those between the greatest grandmasters, are won and lost by mistakes. No matter how brilliantly the World Champion may play he cannot hope to win in the opening unless his opponent plays badly, unless he makes a big mistake or a collection of smaller ones.

All you can do is to learn to recognize the tactical themes which occur over and over again in the opening and to understand the basic rules of opening play. Then at the board you must be alert, ready to pounce the moment your opponent slips ... and not make those same mistakes yourself!

Warning!

In the first part of this book you will learn to recognize the tactical themes, the tricks or traps, the combinations, the points of weakness, which occur over and over again in the opening phase of the game.

Remember! When you spot your chance to use one of these tactical ideas in your own games you must calculate the moves and *make sure it works!* Just because you have seen a brilliant idea in a book doesn't mean it will always work in similar positions in your own games.

Warning!

Rules are made to be broken!

In the second part of this book you will learn the rules of opening play, how to handle your pieces, the importance of time, the importance of the centre and so on.

But rules are only guidelines. In general they should be followed but there are times when they should be broken.

You must learn the rules. You must treat them with respect and break them only when you can see a very good reason for doing so.

Tactical Themes: The Theory

Tactics are fun! They are the tricks or traps in chess which enable us to catch the opponent by surprise and win his pieces or checkmate his king. They are usually a short series of moves which we call combinations and which can be calculated accurately in advance.

There are tactical possibilities in every chess opening. There are some tactical ideas which are special to particular openings but there are others which can occur in almost any opening and those are the ones we are going to concentrate upon here.

We are going to begin by looking at the six most important tactical ideas. You must learn to recognize them. You must learn to spot the chance to use them in your own games.

The h-file Diagonal

In the diagram below two black pawns have been removed to highlight Black's weakness on the diagonal from h5.

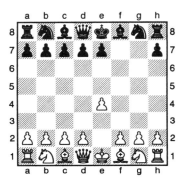

Let's examine Black's position:

a) The diagonal from h5 leads directly to Black's king and the king has no escape square.

b) No black piece can move to g6 to block the diagonal.

c) Only the black king defends the square f7.

d) Only the black knight moving to f6 can easily attack h5.

Clearly Black has no control over the diagonal from h5 to his king.

Indeed a white queen or bishop standing on h5 would give mate!

(White has the same problem if his f- and g-pawns have moved: then the diagonal from h4 leads to his king.)

Target Square f7

This time there's no need to remove any pawns to highlight the weak point.

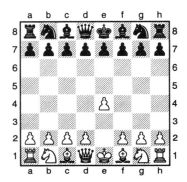

Here we can see:

a) Every pawn from a7 to h7 is defended by a black piece, except the pawn on f7.

b) The square f7 is only defended by the black king.

c) The white queen moving to f3 or h5, the bishop to c4, and the knight to f3 and then e5 or g5 all develop naturally to squares where they can threaten f7.

Clearly Black has little control over f7 whilst it is an easy target for White to attack. A capture on f7 could be mate or it could leave the black king open to further attack.

(Similarly f2 is White's problem square.)

The Open e-file

To appreciate the dangers on the open e-file you will need to apply your imagination to this position:

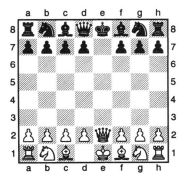

a) First imagine a black knight is on e4. The knight would be pinned against its king, White would play d2-d3 and the knight would be lost.

b) Now imagine that it is a white knight on e4. The knight would be threatening to go to f6 or d6 discovering check from the queen and giving mate.

c) Finally imagine the white knight is on e5. Again there will be a discovered check when the knight moves. The knight can go safely to c6 and win Black's queen or to g6 and win a rook.

Clearly there may be danger when a king is caught by a queen or rook on an open e-file.

Loose Pieces

By the middlegame the pieces have been developed. They usually work together, helping and defending one another. In the opening this is not so. A piece will stride out onto the board, leaving the safety of his comrades at home. Here he will be unprotected, or *'loose'*, and can be a target for attack.

Consider this position:

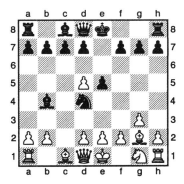

Black has two pieces in play. They look fine but they are both loose and in trouble!

White plays 1 e2-e3 and then:

a) 1...♘d4-f5 2 ♕d1-g4.

b) 1...♘d4-b5 2 ♕d1-a4.

Either way Black's bishop and knight are attacked ... and he can't save both of them!

Clearly pieces that lack support in the opening are targets.

Smothered Mate

In this position there are three things for you to notice:

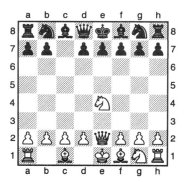

a) White's e-pawn is missing so the e-file is half-open from his side.

b) If the white knight moves, the black e-pawn will be pinned to his king by the white queen.

c) The black king cannot move.

White now has an immediate mate: He can play 1 ♘e4-d6!

The knight cannot be captured because the e-pawn is pinned and the king cannot escape; he is trapped, *smothered* in his bed.

Clearly, for this mate to work, all three conditions above are needed. It doesn't happen often but unless you want to feel as helpless as the black king, you should remember it!

Noah's Ark

This time there are just two points to note:

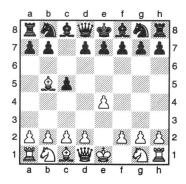

a) The position of the white bishop, who seems alive and healthy.

b) The position of the black c-pawn, who will be the grave-digger.

Black can play 1...a7-a6.

The white bishop may not like to retreat the way he has come but he will be quite safe on c4 or e2. However, if he makes the mistake of going to a4 then he will be buried alive: 2 ♗b5-a4 b7-b5 3 ♗a4-b3 and now the grave-digger nails down the coffin lid with 3...c5-c4.

Clearly, like the smothered mate this is a little tactic which requires special conditions ... but it should be known!

Tactical Themes: The Practice

We have looked at the theory and you now know that f7 is a weak point, that danger lurks on the open e-file ... and so on.

Now we will see how the ideas work in practice by looking at some real games. You must study these games because you can be absolutely sure that you will be able to use the ideas yourself.

But before we begin, remember our warning!

You may see a tactical idea. Maybe there is a queen check on h5. Maybe there is the chance to sacrifice on f7. Maybe the position is exactly the same as one you will see here. Great! Use the tactical idea and win immediately.

But maybe the position is ever so slightly different!

Just because a tactical idea works in one position does not mean it will necessarily work in another ... so be careful! Remember: tactics can be calculated accurately so every time you spot the chance of using one of the tactical ideas in your own games check carefully to make sure it really works ... more often than not it won't!

Fool's Mate

...in which the king is exposed on the h-file diagonal.

The title of Fool's mate is given to:
1   f2-f3   e7-e5
2   g2-g4   ♛d8-h4 mate
It isn't difficult to see where the name came from!

Don't expect many opponents to be generous enough to play 1 f2-f3 and 2 g2-g4 against you, but be aware that the idea of Fool's Mate can arise in other ways:

Bird's Opening
1   f2-f4   e7-e5
2   f4xe5   d7-d6
3   e5xd6   ♝f8xd6
4   ♞b1-c3??   ♛d8-h4+
5   g2-g3

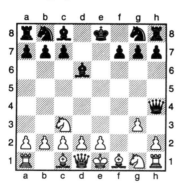

5   ...   ♝d6xg3+
If Black wants to be flash he can capture here with 5...♛h4xg3+ and then mate with the bishop.
6   h2xg3   ♛h4xg3 mate

You should look out for the Fool's Mate idea in any opening where the f-pawn is moved early:

Dutch Defence
1   d2-d4   f7-f5
2   ♝c1-g5   h7-h6
3   ♝g5-h4   g7-g5
The black pawns swarm forward intent on trapping the bishop.
4   ♝h4-g3   f5-f4
And seem to have succeeded.
5   e2-e3
But all is not as it seems! If Black now takes the bishop then the reply 6 ♛d1-h5 is mate.
5   ...   h6-h5
Black prevents the mate and threatens ...h5-h4 trapping the bishop again.
6   ♝f1-d3
With a new mate threat: 7 ♝d3-g6.
6   ...   ♜h8-h6
Black again parries, but now comes the final blow.

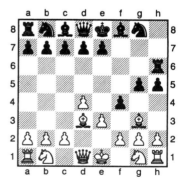

7   ♛d1xh5+!   ♜h6xh5
8   ♝d3-g6 mate
Mate ... and Black never even found time to capture that bishop!

The Knight, e5 and g6

...in which the queen and knight join forces to corner a rook.

Ruy Lopez
1	e2-e4	e7-e5
2	♘g1-f3	♘b8-c6
3	♗f1-b5	♗f8-c5
4	c2-c3	f7-f5

The black f-pawn challenges the centre but the diagonal is opened from h5 to the king.

5	d2-d4	f5xe4
6	♘f3xe5	♗c5-b6?
7	♗b5xc6	d7xc6
8	♕d1-h5+	g7-g6

If Black runs with his king he does not get very far: 8...♔e8-e7 9 ♕h5-f7+ ♔e7-d6 10 ♘e5-c4 mate!

9	♘e5xg6

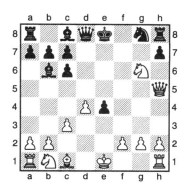

This is the standard type of position. Black loses rook and pawn for knight:

a) 9...h7xg6 10 ♕h5xh8.

b) 9...♘g8-f6 10 ♕h5-e5+ ♔e8-f7 11 ♘g6xh8+.

Do you remember our warning?

Réti's Opening
1	♘g1-f3	♘b8-c6
2	g2-g3	e7-e5
3	e2-e4	f7-f5
4	d2-d4	f5xe4
5	♘f3xe5	♗f8-d6
6	♕d1-h5+	g7-g6
7	♘e5xg6	

All the same as before, only...

7 ...	♘g8-f6

...now the queen dare not check on e5. She has to stay on the h-file or the knight is lost.

8	♕h5-h4

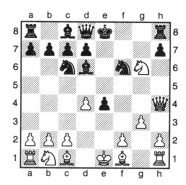

8 ...	♖h8-g8

The rook escapes and...

9	♘g6-f4	♘c6xd4

...it is White, threatened with knight forks on f3 and c2, who loses material.

Remember! You should be aware of the standard tactical ideas but you still have to calculate and make sure they work.

You can't just play moves like 6 ♕d1-h5+ and *expect* them to win for you!

The King-Hunt

...in which the king is exposed on the h-file diagonal and driven to destruction.

King's Gambit Declined
1 e2-e4   e7-e5
2 f2-f4   ♝f8-c5
3 f4xe5??   ♛d8-h4+

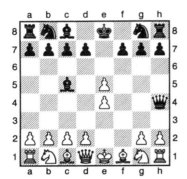

4 ♚e1-e2   ♛h4xe4 mate

Of course, in the diagram position, White can avoid mate. He can play 4 g2-g3. But then follows 4...♛h4xe4+ and 5...♛e4xh1 winning a rook.

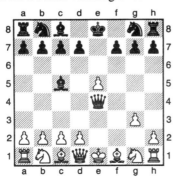

Once the king has been opened up, he is in danger of being driven all over the board:

Centre Game
1 e2-e4   e7-e5
2 d2-d4   f7-f6?

Opening the diagonal from h5 is asking for trouble.

3 d4xe5   f6xe5
4 ♛d1-h5+   ♚e8-e7

After 4...g7-g6 5 ♛h5xe5+ Black loses a rook.

5 ♛h5xe5+   ♚e7-f7
6 ♝f1-c4+   d7-d5

Since 6...♚f7-g6 7 ♛e5-f5 is mate.

7 ♝c4xd5+   ♚f7-g6
8 ♛e5-g3+   ♚g6-h5

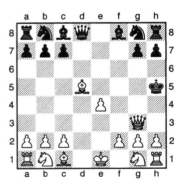

9 ♘g1-f3

Black's position is dreadful, for example:

a) 9...♘g8-f6 10 ♛g3-g5 mate.
b) 9...♝f8-d6 10 ♛g3xg7.
c) 9...♘b8-c6 10 ♝c1-g5.
d) 9...♝c8-g4 10 h2-h3 ♝g4xf3 11 ♛g3xf3+ ♚h5-g6 12 ♝d5-f7 is also mate.
e) 9...Resigns may be best!

The last game was just murder but in a real king-hunt, the chase can be much more exciting!

A. Dubaev v S. Nikitin
Leningrad 1989
Ruy Lopez

1	e2-e4	e7-e5
2	♘g1-f3	♘b8-c6
3	♗f1-b5	f7-f5

This is the Schliemann Defence. Black is looking for a fight but of course he is taking a risk, opening the diagonal to his king. White quickly makes use of this line.

4	♘b1-c3	♘c6-d4
5	e4xf5	c7-c6
6	♘f3xd4	e5xd4
7	♕d1-h5+	♔e8-e7
8	0-0	

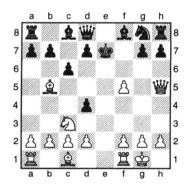

Dubaev is on the attack, but is he winning? Nikitin's king is on the run but two of Dubaev's pieces are attacked and he won't be able to save both of them.

8	...	♘g8-f6
9	♖f1-e1+	♔e7-d6

Unless they had actually played or analysed this position before, it is unlikely that either Dubaev or Nikitin had much idea of what was really going on!

10 ♕h5-h4
Better than 10 ♘c3-e4+ ♘f6xe4 11 ♖e1xe4.

10 ... c6xb5
Better than 10...d4xc3 11 ♕h4-f4+ or 10...♔d6-c7 11 ♕h4xd4.

11	♘c3xb5+	♔d6-c6
12	♕h4xd4	

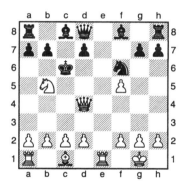

Sacrificing another piece! It is not easy staying calm in such wild positions but the game will be won by the player who keeps his nerve and calculates accurately.

12	...	♔c6xb5
13	a2-a4+	♔b5-c6
14	♕d4-c4+	♗f8-c5
15	♕c4-b5+	♔c6-d6
16	d2-d4	♗c5xd4
17	♗c1-f4+	**Resigns**

Was that the right result? Could Nikitin have saved himself? Spend an hour analysing this game and you will learn an awful lot about king-hunts!

Winning in the Opening

f7 Mates

...in which the weak-point is used for a direct checkmate.

The simplest mate on f7 is known as *Scholar's Mate*:

1	e2-e4	e7-e5
2	&f1-c4	&f8-c5
3	♕d1-h5	♘b8-c6

Black has defended his e-pawn but he has forgotten about the more important f-pawn.

    4 ♕h5xf7 mate

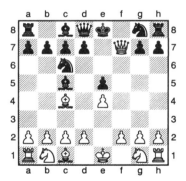

There are other ways of delivering *Scholar's Mate*:

a) 1 e2-e4 e7-e5 2 ♕d1-h5 ♘b8-c6 3 &f1-c4 ♘g8-f6 4 ♕h5xf7 mate.

b) 1 e2-e4 e7-e5 2 ♕d1-f3 &f8-c5 3 &f1-c4 d7-d6 4 ♕f3xf7 mate.

If the checkmate does not come off for White, the direct f7 attack can lead to winning a rook: 1 e2-e4 e7-e5 2 &f1-c4 &f8-c5 3 ♕d1-h5 g7-g6 4 ♕h5xe5+ forking king and rook.

As with *Fool's Mate*, you won't find many people falling for this!

That said, f7 remains the weak point, a target for attack, and here we see an international master overlooking a mate:

Aronin v Kantorovich
Moscow 1960
Sicilian Defence

1	e2-e4	c7-c5
2	♘g1-f3	g7-g6
3	c2-c3	b7-b6
4	d2-d4	&c8-b7
5	&f1-c4	

Now Black sees that he can't capture with 5...&b7xe4 since 6 ♘f3-g5 threatens both 7 &c4xf7 mate and 7 ♘g5xe4. (It is true that 6...d7-d5 defends against both threats, but after 7 &c4-b5+ ♘b8-d7 8 d4xc5 b6xc5 9 f2-f3, Black is in deep trouble.)

5	...	d7-d5
6	e4xd5	&b7xd5
7	♕d1-a4+	&d5-c6?

Black had to try 7...♘b8-c6.

    8 ♘f3-e5!!   **Resigns**

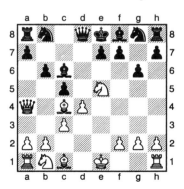

Black loses a piece. Having been given a warning on move 5, he should not have missed the second mate!

Legall's Mate

...in which Black wins a queen but loses his king.

Many of the greatest games of the eighteenth and early nineteenth centuries were played in the grand Café de la Régence in Paris. Sire de M. de Kermur Legall was the café's first great champion but history has remembered him for only one game:

Legall v Saint Brie
Paris c. 1750
Bishop's Opening

1	e2-e4	e7-e5
2	♗f1-c4	d7-d6
3	♘g1-f3	♗c8-g4
4	♘b1-c3	g7-g6
5	♘f3xe5!!	♗g4xd1?

Black is just a pawn down after 5...d6xe5 6 ♕d1xg4 so he greedily gobbles up the queen. Now, however, he is mated!

6	♗c4xf7+	♔e8-e7
7	♘c3-d5 mate	

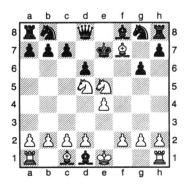

This mating idea crops up in many openings. A variation of it from the Scotch Gambit was chosen by the composers Genee and Zell for a display of living chess in their operetta *The Sea Cadet* in 1889.

A cast of human pieces moving on the stage followed this game played by the Austrian master Ernst Falkbeer:

E. Falkbeer v Amateur
Vienna 1847
Scotch Gambit

1	e2-e4	e7-e5
2	♘g1-f3	♘b8-c6
3	d2-d4	e5xd4
4	c2-c3	d4xc3
5	♘b1xc3	d7-d6
6	♗f1-c4	♗c8-g4
7	0-0	♘c6-e5?
8	♘f3xe5!!	

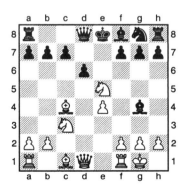

This time Black loses a piece if he doesn't take the queen.

8	...	♗g4xd1
9	♗c4xf7+	♔e8-e7
10	♘c3-d5 mate	

♗xf7+ – The d-file

...in which a bishop is invested for high interest.

The f7/f2 bank can be very generous. For the investment of a bishop, a queen may even be earned:

Petroff Defence
1	e2-e4	e7-e5
2	♘g1-f3	♘g8-f6
3	♘f3xe5	♘b8-c6?!
4	♘e5xc6	d7xc6
5	e4-e5	♘f6-e4
6	d2-d3?	♗f8-c5!

Now White is deep trouble.

7 d3xe4?

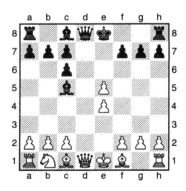

7	...	♗c5xf2+

The bishop is invested. The bank pays the immediate interest of a pawn ... but Black wants more ... and he gets more ... the white queen!

8 ♔e1-e2

8 ♔e1xf2 ♕d8xd1 loses the queen immediately.

8	...	♗c8-g4+
9	♔e2xf2	♕d8xd1

The white queen is a good return for Black's investment!

As always the interest must be thoroughly calculated before the investment is made:

Danish Gambit
1	e2-e4	e7-e5
2	d2-d4	e5xd4
3	c2-c3	d4xc3
4	♗f1-c4	c3xb2
5	♗c1xb2	d7-d5
6	♗c4xd5	

Now if Black plays 6...c7-c6 he is hit by 7 ♗d5xf7+! ♔e8-e7 8 ♗b2-a3+ ♔e7xf7 9 ♕d1xd8, so...

6	...	♘g8-f6
7	♗d5xf7+	

It looks the same ... but it isn't!

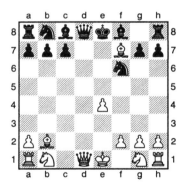

7	...	♔e8xf7!
8	♕d1xd8	♗f8-b4+

And now White will lose a piece unless he returns the queen.

9	♕d8-d2	♗b4xd2+
10	♘b1xd2	

White has regained his original investment ... but no more. Black has won back his queen with a good position.

♗xf7+ – The Queen Fork

...in which the piece is regained with lower interest.

We must not be greedy! Winning the queen on the last page was very nice but with ♗xf7+ we must usually be satisfied with smaller advantages.

Bishop's Opening

1	e2-e4	e7-e5
2	d2-d4	e5xd4
3	♗f1-c4	♗f8-c5
4	♗c4xf7+	♔e8xf7
5	♕d1-h5+	

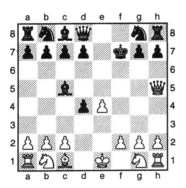

The queen is forking Black's king and loose c5-bishop so White will win back his piece. But what then? The pieces will be equal. So what has White gained? Well:

a) Black's king will not be able to castle. He will get in the way in mid-board and he will be a target for attack.

b) Black will have a lot of trouble defending his d4-pawn.

In the next example it is Black's turn to score on f2:

Ruy Lopez

1	e2-e4	e7-e5
2	♘g1-f3	♘b8-c6
3	♗f1-b5	♗f8-c5
4	♗b5xc6	d7xc6
5	♘f3xe5?	

White wins a pawn but...

5	...	♗c5xf2+!
6	♔e1xf2	

...his knight is loose.

6	...	♕d8-d4+
7	♔f2-e1	♕d4xe5
8	♘b1-c3	c6-c5

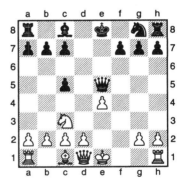

Black has regained his pawn and achieved much more:

a) He has easy development for all of his pieces.

b) He can use the white e-pawn as a target to attack.

c) He has the white king, unable to castle, trapped in the centre.

d) White will have difficulty developing his bishop and rooks.

♗xf7+ – The Knight Check

...in which the knight gives check from g5.

A knight on f3 can be ideally placed to invade after ♗xf7+:

Modern Defence
1 e2-e4   g7-g6
2 d2-d4   ♗f8-g7
3 ♘g1-f3   d7-d6
4 ♗f1-c4   ♘b8-d7?
5 ♗c4xf7+!   ♔e8xf7
6 ♘f3-g5+   **Resigns**

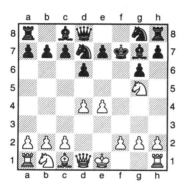

Yes, amazingly Black must resign. The position around Black's king is so cluttered he doesn't have a square for his majesty. Let's look at his three possibilities:

a) 6...♔f7-e8 7 ♘g5-e6 wins the queen.

b) 6...♔f7-f8 7 ♘g5-e6+ forks the black king and queen.

c) 6...♔f7-f6 7 ♕d1-f3 is mate.

When a black bishop stands on g4 the knight can follow up ♗xf7+ with a discovered attack:

Sicilian Defence
1 e2-e4   c7-c5
2 d2-d4   c5xd4
3 c2-c3   d4xc3
4 ♘b1xc3   ♘b8-c6
5 ♘g1-f3   d7-d6
6 ♗f1-c4   ♗c8-g4?

The bishop comes to pin the white knight but the bishop is loose and the pin is not effective.

7 ♗c4xf7+   ♔e8xf7
8 ♘f3-g5+

The knight moves with check so there is no time for the black bishop to take the queen...

8 ...   ♔f7-e8
9 ♕d1xg4

...but there is time for the queen to take the bishop!

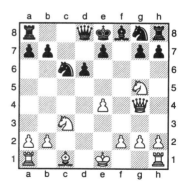

The material is level but White has the advantage because he has better development and Black will have the usual problems with a king which cannot castle.

It's time for another warning!

Altusky v Fischer
Brooklyn 1954
Ruy Lopez

1	e2-e4	e7-e5
2	♘g1-f3	♘b8-c6
3	♗f1-b5	a7-a6
4	♗b5-a4	d7-d6
5	d2-d4	b7-b5
6	♗a4-b3	♗c8-g4?

Now Altusky is all set for the standard bishop sacrifice...

7 ♗b3xf7+??

...only in this position it doesn't work!

7	...	♔e8xf7
8	♘f3-g5+	

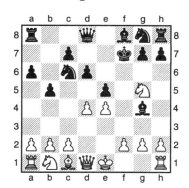

8	...	♕d8xg5!
9	**Resigns**	

When the dust settles, White will be a piece down.

Remember: learn to recognize the tactical themes but in your games, always calculate and check to make sure they work!

Many people reckon Bobby Fischer to have been the greatest player who ever lived. But he played that game when he was eleven, a year or so before "I got good" as he puts it.

7 ♗b3xf7+ didn't work but Bobby's 6...♗c8-g4 was still a mistake. White should have played **7 d4xe5**, reaching this position:

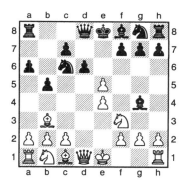

Now Bobby would have had three choices and they are all bad:

a) 7...d6xe5 8 ♕d1-d5 ♕d8xd5 9 ♗b3xd5 ♔e8-d7 10 ♗d5xc6+ ♔d7xc6 11 ♘f3xe5+ winning the bishop on g4.

b) 7...♘c6xe5 8 ♘f3xe5!! ♗g4xd1 9 ♗b3xf7+ ♔e8-e7 10 ♘e5-c6+.

c) 7...♗g4xf3 8 ♗b3xf7+! ♔e8xf7 9 ♕d1-d5+.

Notice how through all the variations the f7-square is a constant target.

The Open e-file and the Discovered Attack

...in which the king is checked and a piece is lost.

Petroff Defence
1 e2-e4   e7-e5
2 ♘g1-f3   ♘g8-f6
3 ♘f3xe5   ♘f6xe4?
4 ♕d1-e2

Attacking the knight and targeting the king.
4 ...   ♘e4-f6??

Black should settle for losing just a pawn by 4...♕d8-e7 5 ♕e2xe4 d7-d6 6 d2-d4. Now...
5 ♘e5-c6+

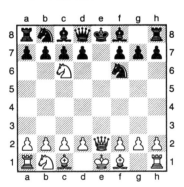

...it is discovered check, the knight is safe from capture, and the black queen is lost. This trap has occurred countless times in games between juniors.

The Open e-file and the Pin

...in which a piece becomes nailed to its king.

A. Zapata v V. Anand
Biel 1988
Petroff Defence

1 e2-e4   e7-e5
2 ♘g1-f3   ♘g8-f6
3 ♘f3xe5   d7-d6
4 ♘e5-f3   ♘f6xe4
5 ♘b1-c3   ♗c8-f5??
6 ♕d1-e2   Resigns

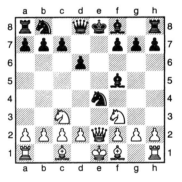

Anand is threatened with 7 d2-d3 winning his pinned knight. He can't escape with 6...♕d8-e7 since 7 ♘c3-d5 hits c7 as well as his queen.

The next time *you* blunder a piece away, take heart! Vishy Anand became a world championship candidate a couple of years after he lost this game. And remember: take care on the e-file!

Smothered Mate

...in which the king dies peacefully in his sleep.

Caro-Kann Defence

1 e2-e4	c7-c6
2 d2-d4	d7-d5
3 ♘b1-c3	d5xe4
4 ♘c3xe4	♘b8-d7
5 ♕d1-e2	

Alarm bells should be ringing furiously in the black king's ears. Why should the white queen develop so early and block the diagonal of her bishop? Sadly...

    5 ...   **♘g8-f6??**

...the king hears nothing...

    6 ♘e4-d6 mate

...and won't ever hear anything again: he's dead!

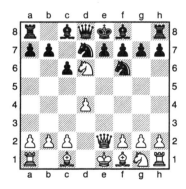

Six moves and the game is over. The black king is surrounded by his courtiers but they give him no comfort at all. Indeed they are just in his way, leaving him with no room to breathe.

That game was the standard form of the smothered mate: king at home, the e-pawn pinned, and the knight giving mate on d6. However, there are other possibilities...

Giuoco Piano

1 e2-e4	e7-e5
2 ♘g1-f3	♘b8-c6
3 ♗f1-c4	♘c6-d4
4 ♘f3xe5?	

It looks as though everything is going great for White. He's won a pawn and has the target f7 in his sights.

    4 ...   **♕d8-g5**

    5 ♘e5xf7

And it still looks fine as Black's queen and rook are forked.

    5 ...   **♕g5xg2**

It doesn't look so good now!

    6 ♖h1-f1

Or 6 ♘f7xh8 ♕g2xh1+ 7 ♗c4-f1 ♕h1xe4+ 8 ♗f1-e2 ♘d4xc2+ 9 ♔e1-f1 ♕e4-h1 mate.

    6 ...   **♕g2xe4+**

    7 ♗c4-e2

7 ♕d1-e2 just loses the queen.

    7 ...   **♘d4-f3 mate**

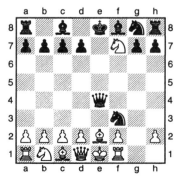

The Loose Queen

...in which her majesty hangs loose centre stage and is unmasked by a bishop.

French Defence

1	e2-e4	e7-e6
2	d2-d4	d7-d5
3	e4-e5	c7-c5
4	c2-c3	♘b8-c6
5	♘g1-f3	♕d8-b6
6	♗f1-d3	

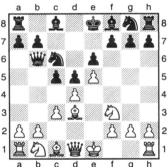

At this point Black does some arithmetic. He counts three pieces, his c-pawn, knight and queen attacking White's d-pawn.

He counts only two white pieces, c-pawn and knight defending. Three is more than two, so he captures...

6	...	c5xd4
7	c3xd4	♘c6xd4?
8	♘f3xd4	♕b6xd4??

Black has got his sums right but the answer is still wrong...

9	♗d3-b5+	♗c8-d7
10	♕d1xd4	**Resigns**

The last game was just opening analysis but even grandmasters can get over-adventurous with their queens in the opening:

T. Ghitescu v R. Fischer
Leipzig Olympiad 1960
Nimzo-Indian Defence

1	d2-d4	♘g8-f6
2	c2-c4	e7-e6
3	♘b1-c3	♗f8-b4
4	e2-e3	0-0
5	♗f1-d3	d7-d5
6	♘g1-f3	♘b8-c6
7	0-0	d5xc4
8	♗d3xc4	♗b4-d6
9	♗c4-b5	e6-e5
10	♗b5xc6	e5xd4
11	e3xd4	b7xc6
12	♗c1-g5	♖f8-e8
13	♕d1-d3	c6-c5
14	d4xc5??	♗d6xh2+

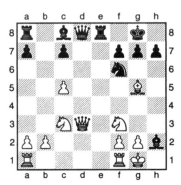

15 Resigns

Which is all rather embarrassing when you are playing top board for your country in an International Team Tournament!

The Pinning Bishop

...in which a bishop finds a pin but is left loose to a fork.

J. Lokvenc v L. Pachman
Prague 1943
Nimzo-Indian Defence

1	d2-d4	♘g8-f6
2	c2-c4	e7-e6
3	♘b1-c3	♝f8-b4

The bishop goes out alone to pin the knight. It should be safe on b4 but it is loose and Black must be careful...

4	♕d1-c2	♘b8-c6
5	♘g1-f3	d7-d6
6	e2-e3	e6-e5
7	d4-d5	♘c6-e7??

He isn't! Of course he should move the knight to e7...

8	♕c2-a4+	Resigns

...but only after he has exchanged his bishop on c3!

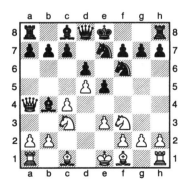

Whichever way Black escapes from check, his bishop falls next move.

In several Queen's Pawn openings, Black must be careful when leaving his bishop loose on b4. In these openings, the problem piece for White can be the bishop on g5:

Queen's Gambit Declined

1	d2-d4	d7-d5
2	c2-c4	e7-e6
3	♘b1-c3	♘g8-f6
4	♝c1-g5	♘b8-d7
5	e2-e3	c7-c6
6	♕d1-c2	♕d8-a5

With this move Black sets a cunning trap.

7	♝f1-d3??

This natural developing move does not look as if it should be a mistake but after...

7	...	d5xc4

...White has both his bishops *en prise*.

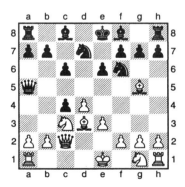

8	Resigns

White loses a piece in view of the following variations:

a) 8 ♝d3xc4 ♕a5xg5.

b) 8 ♝g5xf6 c4xd3 (attacking the queen) 9 ♕c2xd3 ♘d7xf6.

Noah's Ark

...in which a bishop is netted by a pack of pawns.

A. Steiner v J. Capablanca
Budapest 1929
Ruy Lopez

1	e2-e4	e7-e5
2	♘g1-f3	♘b8-c6
3	♗f1-b5	a7-a6
4	♗b5-a4	d7-d6
5	d2-d4	b7-b5
6	♗a4-b3	♘c6xd4
7	♘f3xd4	e5xd4
8	♕d1xd4??	

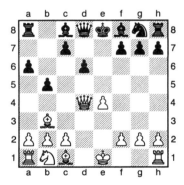

Steiner, who was playing one great world champion, had been reading the words of wisdom of another.

Five years earlier, Alexander Alekhine had recommended this move in a book he had written about a tournament in New York. Great players have great ideas but...

8	...	c7-c5!

...like the rest of us they sometimes make mistakes! The white queen is attacked and when she moves Black will follow up with ...c5-c4 trapping the bishop. White can delay things, fiddling with his queen moves for a couple of moves...

9	♕d4-d5	♗c8-e6
10	♕d5-c6+	♗e6-d7
11	♕c6-d5	c5-c4

...but then the bishop is caught.

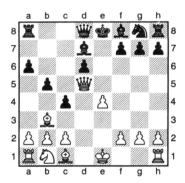

The trap gets its name from the diagonal of black pawns, which are supposed to look like the roof of Mr Noah's biblical boat.

You can learn two good lessons from Steiner's mistake:

1. That a bishop developed to g5 or b5 may be chased away and trapped by an onrushing pack of pawns.

2. That you should never believe everything you read in a book! Even this one! Always check analysis yourself before you play it!

Tactical Themes: The Tests

OK! We've explained the ideas and we've shown how they work in practice.

Now it's your turn to do some work!

On the following pages are thirty-six test positions. The first few are quite easy but they do get much harder as they go on.

You should begin by studying carefully each diagram to try to understand what is happening in the position (the letter *W* or *B* by the diagram will tell you whose turn it is to move).

Look for loose pieces, an attack on f7, tactics on the open e-file and so on.

Then try to answer the question below the diagram.

In each question you will find a clue to help you know what you are looking for. Of course if you are feeling confident and want really to test yourself, you can cover up the questions with a piece of paper, just look at the diagram, see whose turn it is to move and then find the best move. In every position the player to move gets an advantage. This may be checkmate but it may only be the win of a pawn.

(The answers are at the back of the book on pages 124-6)

1. *W*

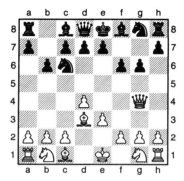

White can checkmate the black king in just two moves. How?

2. *W*

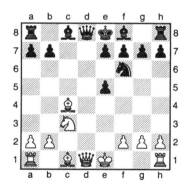

Can you see how White can win the black queen?

3. *W*

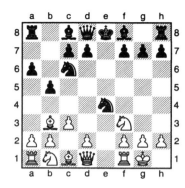

f7 is a target for White's bishop and the e-file is open for his rook. Which of these does he use to win a piece?

4. *B*

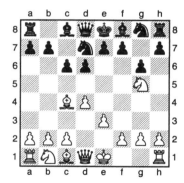

White has just played ♘f3-g5 with a deadly threat of mate on f7. How does Black save himself?

5. *B*

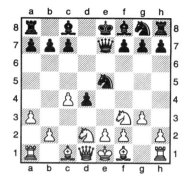

Black's d-pawn is *en prise*. Should he defend it or has he got something better?

7. *W*

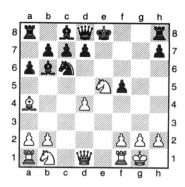

White has a queen check on h5, but does it lead to mate?

6. *W*

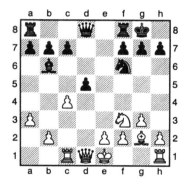

0-0 seems a good idea for White but he has an even better move. What?

8. *W*

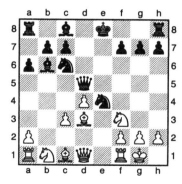

How does White make use of the open e-file?

9. *W*

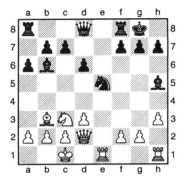

Black's minor pieces are targets for the white pawns. How does White win one of those pieces?

10. *B*

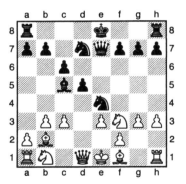

Black's pieces are massed aggressively in the centre. How does he finish the game quickly?

11. *W*

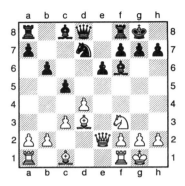

Black has just played ...b7-b6?. Why was this a mistake?

12. *W*

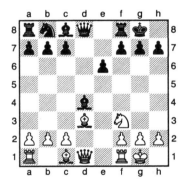

Black has just captured a pawn by ...♗f6xd4. Was this safe?

13. *B*

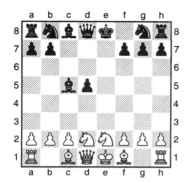

The white king looks warm and cosy in his bed! Black wakes him up and then puts him to sleep permanently! How?

14. *W*

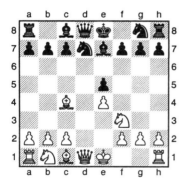

f7 is an obvious target but what is the best way for White to attack?

15. *B*

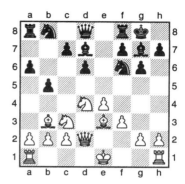

White's pieces seem well placed but a standard trap awaits them. What does Black play?

16. *B*

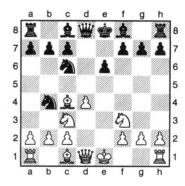

The white queen is overloaded defending c2 and d4. How does Black take advantage?

17. *W*

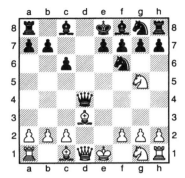

The black queen is loose mid-board but the d3-bishop does not have a check ... yet! What does White play?

18. *W*

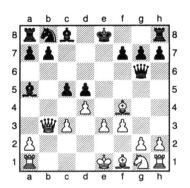

Again, Black has a loose piece. Again, the question is, can White take advantage?

19. *W*

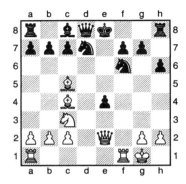

Black has just played ...♘b8-d7. White's bishop on c5 is attacked! What should he do?

20. *B*

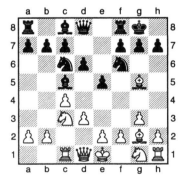

Can you spot the weak point in White's position and how Black takes advantage?

21. *W*

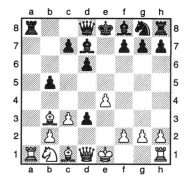

The a-file is open and White's rook is loose. How does he use this to his advantage?

22. *W*

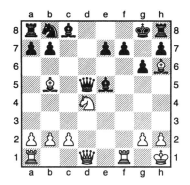

Several pieces are loose but it is the position of the black king which allows White to take advantage. How?

23. *W*

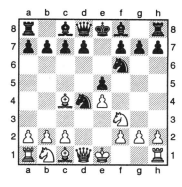

f7 is an inviting target but which is the best way to attack it?

24. *B*

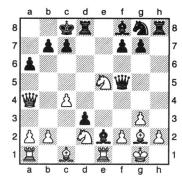

This time a standard tactical idea leads to the threat of mate and enables Black to win material. How?

25. W

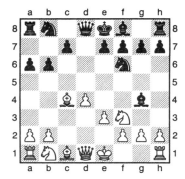

Once again, White can play 1 ♗c4xf7+ but does this work? And is there an even better way of hitting f7?

26. W

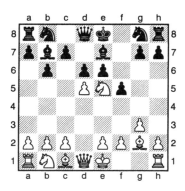

The white knight looks lonely and he's under attack. But does he have to retreat?

27. W

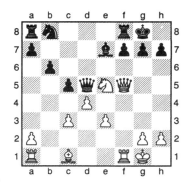

Black's queen and bishop are both loose and his rook is cornered on an open diagonal. How does White take advantage?

28. B

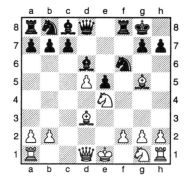

Legall would have approved of Black's move in this position! What is it? And how does Black follow it up?

29. *W*

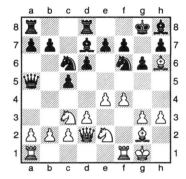

The black king is cornered and the threat of mate will leave the black queen loose. How does White win a piece?

30. *B*

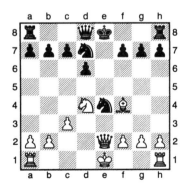

The black knight looks in trouble on the open e-file. Can the piece be saved?

31. *B*

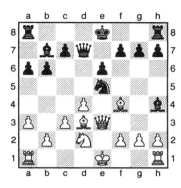

Again Black's knight is in trouble. What does he do about it?

32. *W*

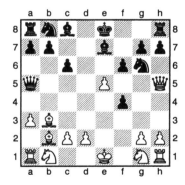

The black queen is loose but how can White take advantage?

33. *B*

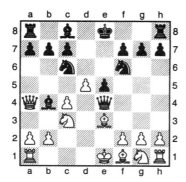

The black knight is pinned and attacked. How does Black turn the tables?

34. *B*

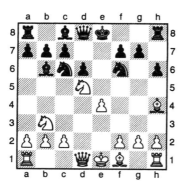

White's bishop is loose on h4 and f2 looks an interesting target. Black can win a pawn. How?

35. *W*

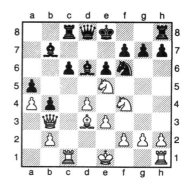

A sacrifice on f7 looks obvious but how does White follow it up?

36. *W*

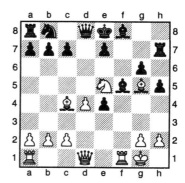

No clues. Just a nice explosion to finish with!

Basic Principles: The Theory

The chessboard is the battlefield. Your pieces are your chess army. You are the general.

A real general starts work long before the battle begins. He has to decide upon the best places to position his men and his heavy weapons so that they will be able to take control of the battlefield and fight effectively.

Your first job in the chess opening is exactly the same. You have to decide upon which squares to place your men so that they too can take control of the battlefield and fight effectively.

To do this properly you must understand the importance of time, space and development: you must learn the ten commandments!

1. Do not expect to be able to attack in the opening.

Your job in the opening is to develop your pieces, to position your men ready for the battle which lies ahead. It is not your job to leap instantly into action and try to batter your opponent to death on the spot.

Play over these moves and you will reach the position in the diagram.

1	e2-e4	e7-e5
2	♗f1-c4	♘b8-c6
3	♕d1-f3	♘g8-f6
4	g2-g4	♗f8-c5
5	g4-g5	♘c6-d4
6	♕f3-d3	♘f6-h5
7	♘g1-f3	♘h5-f4
8	♕d3-c3	♗c5-b4
9	Resigns	

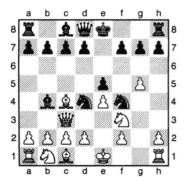

White has lost his queen!

The white queen is attacked. She can't go to a3, b3 or d3 and if she takes the bishop or goes to e3 then she is forked by 9...♘d4xc2+.

Why did this disaster happen?

Because White tried to attack too soon. White played 3 ♕d1-f3. He threatened mate on f7 but Black easily solved that problem.

White was not put off! He continued the attack and tried to renew his threat by advancing his g-pawn but Black just developed his pieces and drove away the white queen.

White's queen and bishop could not force checkmate on their own. When Black answered their threat, they needed the support of the other white pieces to continue the attack. But where were the other white pieces? Nowhere to be seen! They were at home on their starting squares. They were undeveloped.

There will be times when your opponent plays so badly you will be able to take immediate advantage by attacking him. Indeed Black has really done that here. He has improved the position of his knights and bishops, using them to attack and win the white queen. But don't expect this to happen! In the opening your job is to develop your pieces.

Don't start attacking until your pieces are ready for action.

2. Find a good square for a piece, place it there, and don't move it again unless you have a very good reason for doing so.

Development is a race. If you can get your pieces into play quickly you will be able to seize the initiative, you will be ready to attack, you will not have to fear the enemy attacking you. In a race you cannot afford to lose time. In the development race you cannot afford to waste moves.

If you play over these opening moves of the Queen's Gambit, you will reach the position in the diagram:

1	d2-d4	d7-d5
2	c2-c4	e7-e6
3	♘b1-c3	♘g8-f6
4	♗c1-g5	

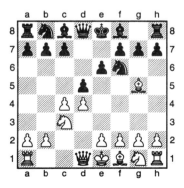

Now it is Black's turn to move.

Suppose Black plays 4...♗f8-e7.
What should White do? Would it be a good idea for White to play 5 ♗g5-f4?
No!
If White wanted his bishop on f4 he should have put it there last move. To move it to f4 now would be waste of time.
But suppose Black plays 4...h7-h6.
Now it is absolutely essential that White moves his bishop for a second time.
And suppose Black plays 4...♘f6-g4, blundering away his queen! Now it is obvious that the advantage gained by 5 ♗g5xd8 is worth the time spent moving the bishop a second time.
Yes, there will be times when you will be forced to move a piece twice in the opening and there will be times when you can gain an immediate advantage by doing so ... but normally you shouldn't!

The general wouldn't give one soldier a gun and tell him to go and fight the enemy army all on his on. If he did, he would soon have one very dead soldier to bury and he wouldn't be ready for the enemy attack. It is the same on the chessboard: you develop *all* of your pieces quickly, you get them into play working together. Then you will be ready to do battle!

3. Place your pieces in, or aiming towards the centre of the board.

Manoeuvrability is a key word to the general. He tries to seize control of the battlefield so that his forces have space and freedom of movement.

For the chess player to seize control of his battlefield he must first control the centre. Pieces placed in, or aiming towards the centre of the board will be more powerful than those on the edge.

Clear your chessboard and take three knights. Place one knight on d4, one on a4 and the other on a8. The knight on d4 is firing in all directions. He attacks and can move to eight squares. The knight on a4 has just four squares and the miserable horse in the corner has just two.

Pieces placed in or towards the centre will not just control more squares, they will have greater freedom to move all over the board.

Let's see what this means in an actual game position.

If you look at the central squares d4, e4, d5 and e5 you will see that White has three pieces aimed at each one of them.

Black attacks d4 and e5 with pawns but does not have a single piece aimed at the centre.

On material, the position is level but White has the advantage as his pieces have tremendous fire-power.

White now has an enormous number of plans to choose from.

a) His c3-knight can go to b5 and hit Black's queen and d-pawn.

b) The knight can go to d5 and hit the queen and the squares e7 and f6.

c) If the knight is on d5, the e1-rook will be able to go to e7 or sacrifice itself on e8 to remove the defending black knight.

d) The g3-bishop can go to h4 hitting the rook and forcing Black to open the diagonal to his king by ...f7-f6.

e) The c2-bishop can go to a4 threatening to win the e8-knight.

f) The white queen can go to f4, g5 or h6 in search of mate.

g) The f3-knight can go to g5 in support of the queen on h6.

White's pieces can literally go wherever they like. Controlling the centre gives his pieces the freedom of the board.

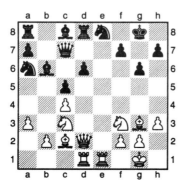

4. Place your pieces so that they work together and help each other.

Co-ordination is another key word for the general. He doesn't just give each of his units a job. He makes sure that they all understand their part in the overall plan. He makes sure that they can work together and help one another when necessary. He makes sure they do not get in each other's way. You must do the same with your chess pieces.

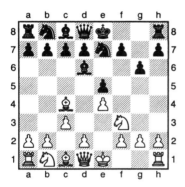

If you look at the position in this diagram, you will see that both players have made two pawn moves, both have moved a bishop and both have moved a knight.

It all sounds the same ... but unfortunately for Black it isn't!

White's pieces are beginning to work together. Black's pieces are beginning to get in each other's way.

Let's make a comparison:

The bishops:
On c4, White's bishop is splendidly placed on the diagonal, hitting at f7. It can be supported by the queen moving to b3 and the knight going to g5.

On d6 Black's bishop is miserably placed on a diagonal where it is blocked by its own pawns on c7 and e5. Worse, Black's bishop simply gets in the way of the d7-pawn which in turn shuts in the c8-bishop and the black queen.

The knights:
On f3, the white knight supports the pawn advance d2-d4 and can move to support the bishop's attack on f7. It also attacks the e5-pawn. On e7, the black knight attacks nothing. It blocks the path of its queen and apart from going home to g8 the only square it has is c6 ... which is the square Black wants for his b8-knight!

The pawns:
On c3, White's pawn is ready to support the d2-d4 advance and has moved to clear the path of the queen from d1 to b3. On g6, Black's pawn is helping nobody. In fact it is just occupying a square the e7-knight could use.

Co-ordination is a key word for the chess player. Develop your pieces so that they can work together in attack and defence.

5. Try to gain time by aggressive development.

Threats have to be answered! If you can develop a piece with a move which carries a little threat, your opponent will have to spend time countering that threat.

In this diagram you can see the position after 1 e2-e4 d7-d5 2 e4xd5 ♛d8xd5.

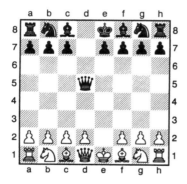

Now White has a developing move which contains a threat.

After 3 ♘b1-c3 Black's queen is attacked. He cannot get on with his development; he must lose a move saving his queen.

Aggressive developing moves can gain time in the race to mobilize and also cut down your opponent's choice of replies.

6. Make only the pawn moves which help with development.

You should remember that pawn moves are not developing moves; they are only an aid to development.

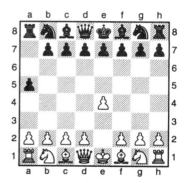

You can see that White has made a good pawn move, Black a bad one:

a) 1 e2-e4 has opened one diagonal for the bishop on f1 and another for the queen. 1...a7-a5 may allow Black to play 2...♖a8-a6 but then the rook would simply be captured.

b) On e4, the white pawn can also help the bishop. White may play 2 ♗f1-c4. Then if the pawn were not on e4 Black would reply with the aggressive 2...d7-d5 and White would lose time running away with the bishop. Black's ...a7-a5 will not help to support his pieces.

c) On e4, the white pawn attacks the important central squares f5 and d5 and prevents Black from developing pieces on those squares. The black a-pawn only attacks the less important side square b4.

7. Remember! Pawns cannot move backwards.

Pawns are important. Their position and movement opens and closes files and diagonals. They also attack and control squares, making them safe for your pieces and preventing your opponent from occupying them.

But remember, unlike the pieces, pawns cannot move backwards. Once a pawn has moved it cannot later retreat to cover a square it has left behind.

In this diagram you can see a pawn skeleton.

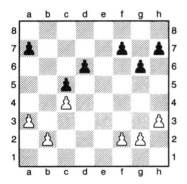

White has three *holes* in his position, b3, d3 and d4, squares where he doesn't have a pawn and which he can never again attack or defend with a pawn. Black has six holes, a5, a6, c6, d5, f6 and h6.

When we add a few pieces to the pawn skeleton we have the position you have seen before on page 44. It is

from a game between Tikhanov and Kapalkin (Leningrad 1987). Most of the holes don't matter but those on d5, f6 and h6 do because White's pieces are ready to invade and Black's are not well placed to defend.

Tikhanov uses all three of them to smash his way to checkmate.

  1   ♘c3-d5!   ♕c7-b7
  2   ♖e1-e7   ♗c8-d7
  3   ♕d2-h6   ♘a6-c7

White was threatening 4 ♖e7xe8+ ♖d8xe8 5 ♘d5-f6+ ♔g8-h8 6 ♕h6xh7 mate...

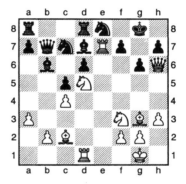

  4   ♖e7xe8+
...it's mate just the same!
  4   ...   ♘c7xe8
  5   ♘d5-e7+   ♔g8-h8
  6   ♕h6-f8 mate

You have to make pawn moves! If you don't you will never control the centre and you will never develop your pieces. But remember that pawn moves leave weak squares behind them. Try not to make holes which you cannot control with your pieces.

8. Beware the danger of pinching pawns!

You must remember that whenever a pawn is captured, a move is spent and a file and diagonals will be opened. You can see this clearly in the position after White's fifth move of the Danish Gambit:

1	e2-e4	e7-e5
2	d2-d4	e5xd4
3	c2-c3	d4xc3
4	♗f1-c4	c3xb2
5	♗c1xb2	

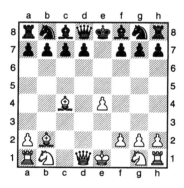

Let's get a set of scales and weigh White's position.

In one pan White has open lines and a lead in development. He will have excellent attacking chances and Black will have to defend carefully.

In the other pan Black has two extra pawns. He has a material advantage in the bank which he may be able to cash in later in the game if White's attack fails.

The scales show a strange sort of balance. Material on one side against development on the other.

Some openings like the Danish above are real gambits in which a player deliberately offers a pawn in exchange for quick development. In other openings the chance to snatch a pawn will also arise.

Before you accept, there are three points to remember:

a) Pawns are only small but they are an important part of the chess army. They are valuable! If you can win a pawn, win it ... so long as you are not taking too big a risk by doing so.

b) The d- and e-pawns are particularly valuable as they take part in the battle for the centre.

c) Time is also valuable, and in the opening time means moves and development. Time spent pinching pawns cannot also be spent developing pieces.

Win a pawn if you can. Put it in the bank! One day it may become a new queen. But don't take risks. Each time you pinch a pawn you spend a move and you are likely to be opening lines for your opponent's pieces. The opening is for developing your pieces ... not pinching your opponent's pawns.

9. Find open files for your rooks.

The rooks are the most difficult pieces to develop. The first problem is that they begin the game stuck away in the corner and the second problem is that their own pawns always seem to get in their way. Let's look at the rooks in the Tikhanov v Kapalkin game.

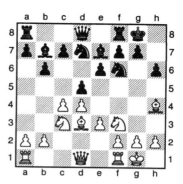

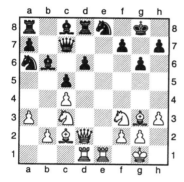

White's e1-rook has a superb base on the open file and you may remember the vital part it played in the mating attack. The d1-rook is also well placed on a half-open file, supporting the attack on Black's d-pawn

In comparison Black's rooks are miserable creatures blocked in behind their own pawns.

To be powerful, rooks need open files! But, how do we know which files will become open? Open files occur when pawns are exchanged so we have to look at the pawn skeleton to get a clue.

In this position White has developed his minor pieces and is now thinking about where to put his rooks. Which rook move should he play?

♖a1-c1 would be a good move. It is easy to see that the white pawn on c4 can be exchanged for the black pawn on d5. When this happens a rook on c1 will have a clear path to c7.

♖f1-e1 would be quite good. It takes a little more imagination, but White might be able to play e3-e4 or Black might play ...c7-c5 and ...c5xd4. In both cases the white e-pawn could capture and the e-file would be opened.

♖a1-b1 does not seem very sensible as it is difficult to see how the white b-pawn is ever going to get out of the rook's way.

Rooks need open lines. If a file is open, seize it. If not, you must study the pawn position and work out where pawns are likely to be exchanged. Then you will know where to put your rooks.

10. Get castled quickly!

Do you remember the warnings in the tactical section at the beginning of this book?

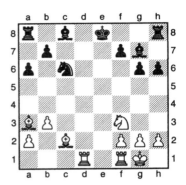

The h-file diagonal (h5-e8 for Black, h4-e1 for White) is a danger spot in the opening because it leads straight to the black king.

f7 is a danger spot because it is right next to the king's square.

The e-file is a danger spot since the king can be trapped on the end of it.

All of this suggests that e8 (or e1 for White) is not a very happy home for the king! The solution though is easy: get castled!

When you castle you achieve three things:

a) You get your king out of the danger area.

b) You hide him away behind a shield of pawns (provided you have not made any rash pawn advances).

c) You bring your rook towards the centre, where it is more likely to find open files.

You can see how all this works out in the position below in another Tikhanov game (against Tetradze in Leningrad 1990):

Firstly, the kings:

Black has not castled. His king has been caught in the centre and is an immediate target for attack. White's king is much safer, tucked away behind a wall of pawns.

Secondly, the rooks:

Black's cower in their corners, but castling has helped the white rooks to team up.

Working together they power down the central files.

Finally, the result!

Even without the queens the game came to a sudden, violent and rather beautiful end: **1 ♖f1-e1+ ♗c8-e6 2 ♖e1xe6+! f7xe6 3 ♗c2xg6 mate**.

The king needs safety, the rooks need open files and work well when they come together. So get castled!

Basic Principles: The Practice

We have looked at the theory and you have read the commandments. You know about the importance of time, rapid development and the centre. You know that rooks need open files, that you should castle quickly and that you should try to catch your opponent's king in the centre.

Now is the time to look at some real games and see what can happen to players who are tempted to break the rules. In all of our games the loser is punished quickly for his mistakes: all of the games are short and most end in a bloodbath with the winner sacrificing brilliantly or simply hacking his opponent to bits.

You will also see that our tactical themes crop up over and over again and that somehow it always seems to be the player who falls behind in development, neglects the centre or who fails to castle who gets caught in a tactical trap.

You will look at many of the games and think 'I wish I could play a game like that!' Well, you can! Learn the commandments, play over the games and learn how to spot the mistakes and you too will be able to take quick advantage.

Game 1

...in which Black learns that just one little error can cause total disaster.

S. Tarrasch v J. Taubenhaus
Nuremberg 1892
Ruy Lopez

1	e2-e4	e7-e5
2	♘g1-f3	♘b8-c6
3	♗f1-b5	a7-a6
4	♗b5-a4	♘g8-f6
5	0-0	♘f6xe4
6	d2-d4	b7-b5
7	♗a4-b3	d7-d5
8	d4xe5	

And we have a position which has been reached in thousands of games. Black now usually plays 8...♗c8-e6 as this:

a) defends the pawn on d5.

b) brings the bishop into play.

c) means that the black rook which was loose on a8 is now protected by the queen.

That's what Black should have done. However, he had a bright new idea of his own...

8 ...   ♘c6-e7?

Black doesn't think a piece should be tied up defending a pawn. He plans to play ...c7-c6, ...♘e7-g6, ...♗f8-e7, put his bishop on f5 or g4, and castle his king into safety.

A great idea ... but a dreadful move! With 8...♘c6-e7 he:

a) wastes time moving his knight once again.

b) blocks the path of his bishop on f8.

c) makes it more difficult for himself to castle.

d) moves the knight away from the centre, where it was well placed attacking the important squares e5 and d4.

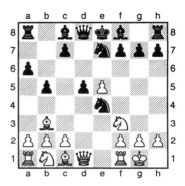

Now, the important question. White has spotted his opponent's error but how should he take advantage?

First he should look for an immediate combination. Maybe a tactical trick to get at the black king. There isn't one, so he should try to seize the initiative. He should continue to develop but he should try to play forcefully.

9 a2-a4!

White doesn't intend to give Black the time to carry out his plan. Immediately he threatens 10 a4xb5 when Black will lose his rook if he recaptures.

9 ...   ♗c8-e6

Black admits failure! After 9...c7-c6 10 a4xb5 c6xb5 his d-pawn looks sick and will need help from the bishop anyway.

10 ♕d1-e2

The queen finds two paths of attack. On the diagonal she hits b5 again. On the file she eyes the black king hidden but trapped behind the clutter of pieces.

10	...	c7-c6
11	c2-c3	♘e7-g6
12	♘f3-d4!	

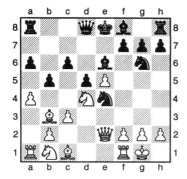

Great! The knight swipes in all directions, most importantly at c6. At the same time the way is cleared for the white f-pawn to snap menacingly up the board at the black minor pieces.

| 12 | ... | ♗e6-d7 |

Oh dear! Again Black loses time moving a piece twice, but what else could he do? If 12...♕d8-d7, 13 a4xb5 c6xb5 14 ♘d4xb5 and he will lose a rook if he recaptures.

13	a4xb5	a6xb5
14	♖a1xa8	♕d8xa8
15	♗b3-c2	

Now Black has to answer the threat of 16 ♗c2xe4 d5xe4 17 ♕e2xe4. He just never has the time to untangle himself.

| 15 | ... | ♘e4-c5 |

Black has major trouble on the e-file because his king is stuck in the centre. If he tries either 15...♘g6xe5 16 f2-f3 or 15...f7-f5 16 e5xf6 g7xf6 17 f2-f3 then the pin will cost him a knight.

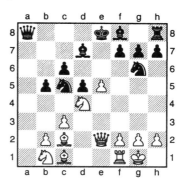

| 16 | f2-f4 | |

The terrier is let loose.

| 16 | ... | ♗f8-e7 |

Development, but too late!

| 17 | f4-f5 | |

Snap!

| 17 | ... | ♘g6-f8 |
| 18 | f5-f6 | |

Snap!

| 18 | ... | g7xf6 |
| 19 | e5xf6 | |

And snap again!

| 19 | ... | **Resigns** |

The f-pawn has chewed up Black's kingside and there's no way of saving the bishop.

White just seized the initiative. From move 9 he played a series of forcing moves which never gave Black a hope of sorting out his muddle and getting developed.

Game 2

...in which Black walks into a trap and White finds that it isn't a trap after all.

E. Schiffers v M. Chigorin
St Petersburg 1878
Ruy Lopez

1	e2-e4	e7-e5
2	♘g1-f3	f7-f5
3	e4xf5	♘b8-c6
4	♗f1-b5	

The order of the moves is unusual but the opening is the risky Schliemann Defence to the Ruy Lopez. Black hopes to develop his pieces quickly and actively but he has opened the diagonal to his king and is inviting trouble.

4	...	♗f8-c5
5	♗b5xc6?	

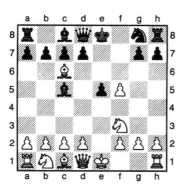

White's eyes have lit up! He has seen that he will be able to capture with his knight on e5. He has seen that his queen can come to h5 with check. He has seen that the black king will be in trouble. And he has seen that the black bishop will be loose on c5. However, there is something he hasn't seen ... yet!

5	...	d7xc6

This was the drawback of White's last move. In capturing the bishop Black has been able to open the d-file for his queen and the diagonal for his queen's bishop.

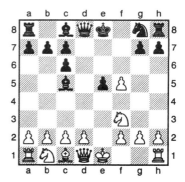

6	♘f3xe5	♗c8xf5
7	♕d1-h5+	g7-g6
8	♘e5xg6	

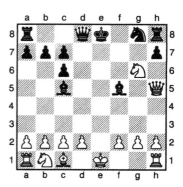

White is still happy. Everything has gone according to plan. His queen and knight are on the rampage, the black king is wide open and the black rook looks doomed.

Black cannot play 8...♗f5xg6 since his other bishop is loose and he will just be two pawns down after 9 ♕h5xc5. So...

8	...	h7xg6
9	♕h5xh8	

...just as White had foreseen, Black has been caught in the standard opening trap and lost the exchange and a pawn.

9	...	♕d8-e7+

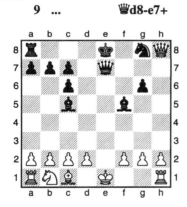

This is the start of what White had not seen!

The complications are over and Black has his queen powering down the centre and his bishops supplying crossfire on open diagonals. White has won material but he has exchanged his only two developed minor pieces and now he has only his queen in play.

10 ♔e1-d1

White only has a choice of which way to lose.

After the alternative 10 ♔e1-f1 ♗f5xc2 11 ♕h8xg8+ ♔e8-d7 he can choose between:

a) 12 ♕g8xa8 ♗c2-d3+ 13 ♔f1-g1 ♕e7-e1 mate; and

b) 12 ♕g8-c4 ♖a8-e8 13 g2-g3 ♕e7-e1+ 14 ♔f1-g2 ♕e1xf2+ with a quick mate.

10	...	♗c5xf2!
11	♕h8xg8+	♔e8-d7
12	♕g8-c4	

White doesn't have time to capture the rook as he must prevent 12...♗f5-g4 mate...

12	...	♖a8-e8

...but he is mated anyway. Black's last piece springs into action on the open file and mate is threatened by 13...♕e7-e1+ 14 ♖h1xe1 ♖e8xe1.

13 Resigns

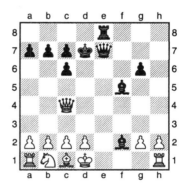

If 13 d2-d3, 13...♕e7-e2 is mate whilst 13 d2-d4 ♗f5-g4+ 14 ♔d1-d2 ♕e7-e3 is also death.

White made a common mistake. He saw his chance and he went for it. He saw the standard trap and he grabbed the exchange.

In his excitement he didn't look further. He never saw the danger ... until it hit him!

Game 3

...in which the black queen gets lost in the crowd.

G. Kluger v Nagy
Budapest 1942
Sicilian Defence

1	e2-e4	c7-c5
2	♘g1-f3	♘b8-c6
3	d2-d4	c5xd4
4	♘f3xd4	♘g8-f6
5	♘b1-c3	d7-d6
6	♗c1-g5	a7-a6
7	♕d1-d2	♘f6-d7?

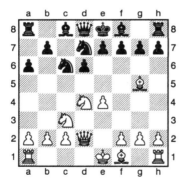

This is a really awful move! It:

a) moves a piece unnecessarily for a second time.

b) places the piece on a square where it blocks the lines of both the queen and bishop.

c) takes the knight away from the centre where it was attacking White's e-pawn and the important square d5.

It's not easy trying to find a sensible reason for the black knight's retreat. If Black had plans for the knight

on c5 or e5 he should first have completed his development. 7...e7-e6 followed by ...♗f8-e7 and ...0-0 would have been much better.

8	♗f1-e2	g7-g6
9	♘c3-d5	

And what is this? Now we have White breaking the rules! Surely he should castle and not waste time moving the knight again?

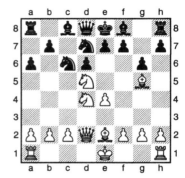

White is setting a really nasty trap and since he has such a big lead in development and his pieces are so powerfully placed in the centre he can afford the luxury of moving the knight twice in order to seize the initiative.

9	...	f7-f6?

Another awful move, leaving a hole on e6. But what else could Black have done?

If he had continued with his intended plan of 9...♗f8-g7 he would have lost his queen after 10 ♘d4xc6 b7xc6 11 ♗g5xe7 since there is not a single safe square for the poor lady.

Things are just as bad if he tries to avoid this by chasing away the white bishop: after 9...h7-h6 10 ♗g5-h4 g6-g5 he has shut out the bishop but

White has the startling move 11 ♘d4-e6!!...

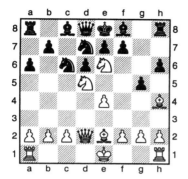

...when Her Majesty is in yet more trouble. Then:

a) 11...f7xe6 12 ♗e2-h5 gives us the familiar mate on the king's diagonal.

b) 11...♕d8-a5 12 ♕d2xa5 ♘c6xa5 13 ♘d5-c7 gives a very pretty mate with the two knights.

The best hope for Black would be to take some of the pressure off his position by exchanging: after 9...♘c6xd4 10 ♕d2xd4 White still has a big lead in development and his pieces control the centre but at least he can't embarrass the black queen with ♘d4-e6.

So now back to the game with:

10 ♘d4-e6

Of course!

10 ... ♕d8-a5

This time the queen is able to find safety ... unfortunately her royal partner will not be so lucky.

11 ♘d5-c7+ ♚e8-f7
12 ♘e6-d8+ ♚f7-g7

Here Black had two other possibilities:

a) 12...♚f7-g8 13 ♗e2-c4+ is similar to the game and will cost him his king.

b) 12...♘c6xd8 13 ♕d2xa5 and the queen falls yet again.

13 ♘c7-e8+ ♚g7-g8
14 ♗e2-c4+ Resigns

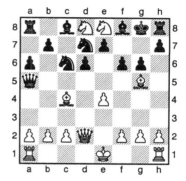

When Black has run out of things to put in the way and White has finished capturing them it will be mate!

All of Black's trouble was caused by the wretched knight which parked itself on d7 and did nothing for the rest of the game but get in the way.

Of course 9 0-0 or 9 0-0-0 would have been fine but White realized Black's position was so cluttered and undeveloped that he could afford to break the rules, move the knight again, and get the job finished.

Game 4

...in which White finds a hole and digs in deep.

Y. Tikhanov v M. Piatrovsky
Leningrad 1990
Vienna Gambit

1	e2-e4	e7-e5
2	♘b1-c3	♗f8-b4
3	f2-f4	♗b4xc3

Black is playing to shatter White's pawn structure but on an open board where pieces can move around freely, bishops are generally considered better than knights.

4 d2xc3   e5xf4

Black has achieved his aim. White has doubled pawns on the c-file and his e-pawn is isolated and weak. But Tikhanov, giving a simultaneous exhibition, is not at all worried: with open lines and easy development he plans to blow his opponent away at high speed.

5 ♘g1-f3   c7-c6?

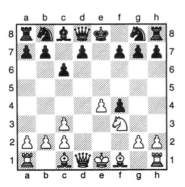

Black intends to challenge the centre with ...d7-d5. Normally this would be a good idea but here there are two problems:

a) He is leaving a nasty hole on d6 in a position where he has already exchanged his dark-squared bishop.

b) White doesn't have any intention of allowing him to play ...d7-d5.

6	♗f1-c4	♘g8-e7
7	♕d1-d6	

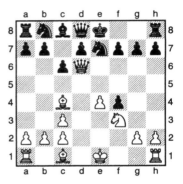

White occupies the hole. If Black can't move his d-pawn, he is going to have great problems developing his queenside pieces.

7 ...   0-0?

7...♘e7-g6 and 8...♕d8-e7 is a better way of fighting for the dark squares. If White plays 8 ♗c1xf4 then Black will be only too happy to exchange his knight for the dark-squared bishop.

8	♗c1xf4	♘e7-g6
9	♗f4-g5	♕d8-e8
10	0-0	♕e8xe4

White's lead in development is overwhelming so Black looks to fight back by grabbing a pawn and attacking the c4-bishop. Of course, he shouldn't be pinching a pawn and he doesn't really want to open the e-file since it is White's a1-rook which will soon seize the open line.

11 &f3-d4 &e4-e5
12 &d4-f5!

The knight defends the queen, prepares to occupy the hole and carries the deadly threat of 13 &f5-e7+ &g8-h8 14 &e7xg6+ winning the black queen.

12 ... &g8-h8
13 &g5-e7 &e5xd6

Since 13...&g6xe7 blunders away the queen and the alternative 13...&f8-e8 14 &a1-e1 &e5xd6 15 &f5xd6 &e8xe7 16 &d6xf7+ leaves him totally splattered.

14 &e7xd6

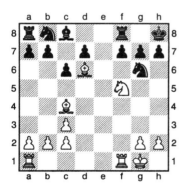

The exchange of queens has done nothing to help Black. His d-pawn is still fixed, he is a long way behind in development and White's minor pieces are walking all over him.

14 ... &f8-d8

Grabbing the open file looks more sensible but after 14...&f8-e8 15 &c4xf7 &e8-e2 16 &a1-e1 it is White

who is going to control the file and who will have horrible threats on the end of it.

15 &c4xf7 b7-b6

At last Black gets around to doing something about his queenside development. Too late! He's about to be checkmated.

16 &f1-f3! &c8-a6
17 &f7xg6 h7xg6
18 &f3-h3+ &h8-g8
19 &f5-e7+ &g8-f7

Or 19...&g8-f8 20 &h3-f3+ &f8-e8 21 &e7xg6 and mate next move.

20 &a1-e1!

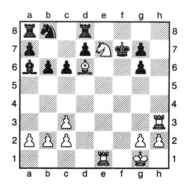

Development complete! Tikhanov threatens mate after 21 &h3-f3+ &f7-e8 22 &e7xg6+.

20 ... &f7-f6
21 &h3-f3+ &f6-g5
22 &e1-e5+ &g5-g4
23 h2-h3+ &g4-h4
24 &e7xg6 mate

Now we have a second hole: h4 is Black's grave! White meanwhile is still dug in deep on d6!

Game 5

...in which the white king dallies in the centre and Black makes sure he stays there.

D.E. Lloyd v K. Darga
Bognor Regis 1960
Sicilian Defence

1	e2-e4	c7-c5
2	♘g1-f3	e7-e6
3	c2-c4	♘b8-c6
4	d2-d4	c5xd4
5	♘f3xd4	♘g8-f6
6	♘b1-c3	♗f8-b4
7	♕d1-d3?	

Black was threatening 7...♘f6xe4 but ♕d1-d3 is a poor way to defend. On d3 the queen is blocking the line of her bishop and is a sitting target for an attack by a black knight. Better is 7 ♘d4xc6 b7xc6 8 ♗f1-d3.

7 ...   0-0
Black puts his king into safety and prepares ...♖f8-e8.

8 ♘d4-c2?
A dreadful waste of time. The knight has made three moves and if he makes a fourth, capturing the bishop, Black will simply recapture with the knight and gain more time attacking the white queen.

8 ...   d7-d5!
White is still two moves away from castling. Black immediately seizes his chance to smash open the e- and d-files and catch the king in the centre. Black threatens both 9...d5-d4 and 9...♘f6xe4, so White must exchange.

9 e4xd5   e6xd5

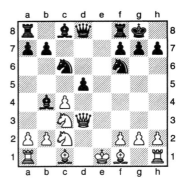

10	c4xd5	♘f6xd5
11	♗c1-d2	

White would have loved to have been able to remove the black bishop but after 11 ♘c2xb4 Black could have retaken with either knight. Then he would have been attacking the queen and threatening to fork on c2.

11 ...   ♖f8-e8+

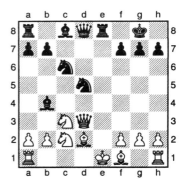

Black has caught the white king in the centre. Now his task will be to keep him there.

12	♗f1-e2	♗b4xc3
13	b2xc3	

Recapturing with the bishop looks more reasonable but then Black can immediately make use of the open e-file: 13 ♗d2xc3 ♘d5-f4! and the bishop on e2 is lost.

13 ...   ♗c8-g4
14 ♗d2-e3

This time White would have loved to have driven the bishop away with 14 f2-f3 but 14...♘c6-e5! 15 ♕d3-b5 ♘e5xf3+ 16 g2xf3 ♗g4xf3 is horrible.

14 ...   ♗g4xe2
15 ♕d3xe2

Forced since 15 ♔e1xe2 ♘d5-f4+ wins the queen.

15 ...   ♘d5-f4
16 ♕e2-g4   ♘c6-e5!

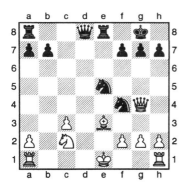

White must not be given time to castle so with every move comes a new threat. The queen is attacked and she cannot capture on f4 because of the fork ...♘e5-d3+.

17 ♕g4-g3   ♕d8-d5!
18 ♖h1-g1

An awful move to have to play! But what else? Let's see:

a) 18 0-0? ♘f4-e2+ wins White's queen.

b) 18 ♗e3xf4 ♘e5-f3++ 19 ♔e1-f1 ♕d5-d3 wins his king.

c) 18 ♖a1-d1 ♘f4xg2+ 19 ♔e1-e2 ♕d5-b5+ 20 ♔e2-d2 ♘e5-c4+ 21 ♔d2-e2 ♘c4xe3+ wins most of his army.

18 ...   ♖a8-d8

Black's pieces co-ordinate beautifully! He has total control of the central files and the white king has no hope of finding safety.

19 ♘c2-d4   ♕d5-c4

Threatening both 20...♕c4xc3+, and 20...♖d8xd4 followed by 21...♕c4-e2 mate.

20 ♗e3xf4   ♘e5-f3++

The double check is a killer!

21 ♔e1-d1   ♕c4xc3
22 Resigns

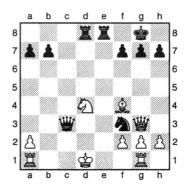

The white king dies mid-board: a fair punishment for not getting castled!

Game 6

...in which the white queen takes a long trip to nowhere.

Astfalk v Mellerovich
Oranienbaum 1989
Queen's Gambit, Tarrasch

1	d2-d4	d7-d5
2	c2-c4	e7-e6
3	♘b1-c3	c7-c5
4	c4xd5	c5xd4!?

The Austrian Anton Schara was the first to play this risky gambit. The normal move is 4...e6xd5 opening the line of the light-squared bishop.

    5   ♕d1xd4   ♘b8-c6!

Schara's idea was to lure the white queen into mid-board and gain developing time by attacking her.

6	♕d4-d1	e6xd5
7	♕d1xd5	♗c8-e6

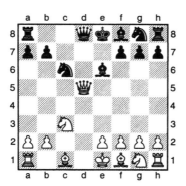

White should now exchange the queens.

After 8 ♕d5xd8+ ♖a8xd8 Black has a two-move lead in development as compensation for his pawn but his

attacking chances are much less with the queens off the board.

However...

    8   ♕d5-b5?

...the white queen sets off in search of glory ... all on her own.

    8   ...   a7-a6

Black realizes that without support the queen cannot do him any real harm so he gets on with his own plans...

    9   ♕b5xb7   ♘c6-b4

...and immediately threatens mate with ...♘b4-c2.

    10 ♕b7-e4   ♘g8-f6

Aggressive development. It is easy to see that it is Black who has more pieces in play and therefore Black who has the initiative.

    11 ♕e4-b1

The queen flees for cover but every move she makes is a move White cannot spend developing his pieces.

    11 ...   ♖a8-c8

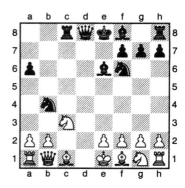

Compare this diagram with the one after move seven and spot the difference! Black has developed one knight and improved the position of the other and he has developed a rook. White has pinched a pawn and transferred his queen from d5 to b1. The queen has made seven moves just to finish holed-up in the corner. The extra pawns would be useful if it came to an endgame but White won't live that long.

12 a2-a3?

Obviously it is tempting to drive away the annoying knight but Black doesn't have an instant threat so White would have done better to begin developing some pieces. And in any case...

12 ... ♗e6-b3!

...he isn't driving the knight away! Black just carries on improving the position of his pieces and occupies the hole.

13 a3xb4 ♖c8xc3!

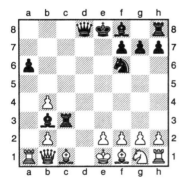

Mate is threatened by 14...♕d8-d1 so White doesn't have time to capture the rook.

14 ♗c1-d2 ♖c3-c2

Now mate is threatened on d2.

15 ♘g1-f3

Development at last! Too late of course.

15 ... ♘f6-e4

The knight leaps into action reinforcing the attack on d2 and finding a new target ... the f2-square.

16 ♗d2-c3 ♗f8xb4!

Black has his pieces working well together, swarming all over White's defences.

17 ♗c3xb4

He had to prevent 17...♘e4xc3.

17 ... ♕d8-b6

18 Resigns

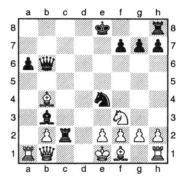

Black threatens both ...♕b6xb4+ and ...♕b6xf2+ and when the white king is driven to d1 there will be a deadly discovered check to finish things off.

Black met White's queen attack with straightforward development and overwhelmed his opponent.

The queen may be the most powerful piece but unless a careless mistake is made she will never win a battle on her own!

Game 7

...in which White avoids opening theory but also forgets the basic principles.

B. Larsen v B. Spassky
Belgrade 1970
Larsen's Opening

1 b2-b3
This game was played on the top board of a match between the Soviet Union and the Rest of the World at a time when Boris Spassky was World Champion and Bent Larsen ranked alongside Bobby Fischer as the number one western player.

Whilst most modern grandmasters know and often follow opening theory for twenty moves or more Bent Larsen likes to get away from the books and lead his opponent down unexplored paths.

1	...	e7-e5
2	♗c1-b2	♘b8-c6
3	c2-c4	♘g8-f6

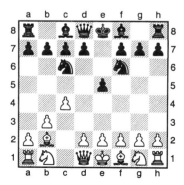

4 ♘g1-f3?

There is no harm in being original but you must keep the basic principles in mind!

| 4 | ... | e5-e4 |
| 5 | ♘f3-d4 | ♗f8-c5 |

Attacking development gains time!

| 6 | ♘d4xc6 | d7xc6 |

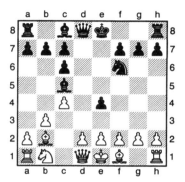

Comparing this with the previous diagram we can see that Black has made progress. He has developed one bishop and opened the diagonal for the other and the file for his queen. White has simply *lost* the knight from g1.

| 7 | e2-e3 | ♗c8-f5 |
| 8 | ♕d1-c2 | |

When he played 4 ♘g1-f3 Larsen was probably imagining that the black pawn lured forward to e4 would become a weakness, a target he could attack. In the long term he might be right ... but Spassky ensures that this is a game without a long term!

| 8 | ... | ♕d8-e7 |
| 9 | ♗f1-e2 | 0-0-0 |

Spassky has met Larsen's ambitious experiment with simple development and now his forces stand ready for action.

10 f2-f4?

White's position cannot stand the luxury of another pawn move, particularly one that weakens the h4-e1 diagonal. 10 ♗b2xf6 followed by 11 ♘b1-c3 would have been more consistent with his plan and helped with development.

10 ...   ♘f6-g4!
11 g2-g3

It isn't easy finding a good move for White! The logical developing moves 11 ♘b1-c3 and 11 0-0 are both met by 11...♖d8xd2!, after which e3 collapses and White's king and queen are in all sorts of trouble. The greedy 11 ♗b2xg7 ♖h8-g8 simply loses time and gives Black an open file.

11 ...   h7-h5!

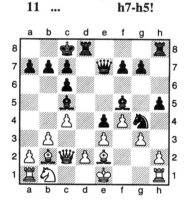

Black has an obvious advantage in development and the white king is stuck in the centre. If Spassky is to make use of his advantage he must smash open lines so that his heavy pieces can get at that king.

12 h2-h3   h5-h4!

Larsen had probably been hoping for 12...♘g4-f6 when the pressure on e3 is relieved and he can answer 13...h5-h4 with 14 g3-g4. Spassky, however, only has one thought in mind: open lines and catch the king!

13 h3xg4   h4xg3
14 ♖h1-g1

Miserable though it is, White's rook is the only piece which can hope to defend its king. 14 ♖h1xh8 ♖d8xh8 15 g4xf5 ♖h8-h1+ 16 ♗e2-f1 g3-g2 mates.

14 ...   ♖h8-h1!!

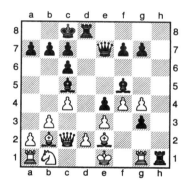

15 ♖g1xh1

Or 15 ♔e1-f1 ♖h1xg1+ 16 ♔f1xg1 ♕e7-h4 and mate in two.

15 ...   g3-g2
16 ♖h1-f1

Or 16 ♖h1-g1 ♕e7-h4+ 17 ♔e1-d1 ♕h4-h1, etc.

16 ...   ♕e7-h4+
17 ♔e1-d1   g2xf1=♕+
18 Resigns

Larsen is mated after 18 ♗e2xf1 ♗f5xg4+ 19 ♔d1-c1 ♕h4-e1+.

With his queenside still undeveloped he was a victim of his own invention!

Game 8

...in which too many pawn moves lead to too many king moves.

A. Novopashin v Y. Berlov
Samara 1994
Philidor's Defence

1	e2-e4	e7-e5
2	♘g1-f3	d7-d6
3	d2-d4	f7-f5

Known as Philidor's Counter-Attack, this move is considered by theory to be risky.

| 4 | ♗f1-c4 | h7-h6? |

This move is not considered by theory and is total madness! It is Black's fourth pawn move and it loses control of g6.

5 ♘f3xe5!

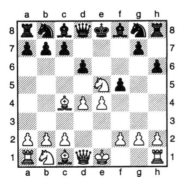

White wastes no time. He opens the line for his queen to seize the diagonal from h5. Of course Black can take the knight but White has calculated that at the very worst he will get three pawns as compensation.

| 5 | ... | d6xe5 |

6 ♕d1-h5+

If Black had not played 4...h7-h6 he could meet this check by 6...g7-g6.

| 6 | ... | ♔e8-d7 |

The king begins his journey and he doesn't have much of a choice of squares. He is mated after 6...♔e8-e7 7 ♕h5-f7+ ♔e7-d6 8 ♕f7-d5+ ♔d6-e7 9 ♕d5xe5+ ♔e7-d7 10 ♕e5-e6.

| 7 | ♕h5xf5+ | ♔d7-c6 |
| 8 | ♕f5xe5 | a7-a6 |

Another pawn move but White was threatening mate beginning with 9 ♕e5-b5+.

| 9 | d4-d5+ | ♔c6-b6 |
| 10 | ♗c1-e3+ | |

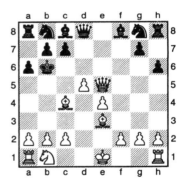

Now the black king is being hunted down he must not be allowed to hide himself away on a7.

| 10 | ... | ♗f8-c5 |

At long last Black manages to develop a piece...

| 11 | ♗e3xc5+ | |

...and White promptly removes it!

| 11 | ... | ♔b6xc5 |
| 12 | d5-d6+! | |

The black king is in real trouble and his undeveloped pieces are in no position to help.

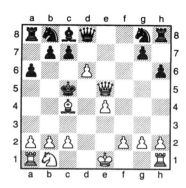

12 ... ♘c5-b6

Taking the bishop leads to immediate mate: 12...♘c5xc4 13 ♛e5-d5+ ♘c4-b4 14 a2-a3+ ♘b4-a4 15 b2-b3.

13 ♛e5xg7

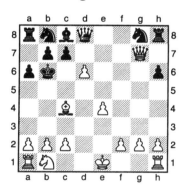

It might be thought that White is breaking the rules with so many queen moves but he is far ahead in development and every queen move carries a powerful threat.

13 ... ♛d8-f6

If 13...♘g8-f6, 14 d6xc7! and the black queen, which is already trying to defend a rook and a knight, has a new problem.

14	♛g7xc7+	♘b6-a7
15	♛c7-c5+	b7-b6
16	♛c5xc8	

With the threat of instant mate on c7.

| 16 | ... | ♛f6-g7 |
| 17 | ♝c4-d5 | |

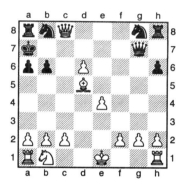

17 ... **Resigns**

White is set to add more material to his prize hoard of five pawns.

Too many pawn moves and a fatal weakness on the diagonal from h5.

Novopashin would not have worked everything out when he played 5 ♘f3xe5. Instinct would have told him that without piece support the black king could not survive in mid-board.

Game 9

...in which Black crumples quickly after a collection of small errors.

Salm v Garner
Correspondence World Championship 1959-61
Petroff Defence

1	e2-e4	e7-e5
2	♘g1-f3	♘g8-f6
3	♘f3xe5	d7-d6
4	♘e5-f3	♘f6xe4
5	d2-d4	d6-d5
6	♗f1-d3	♗f8-e7
7	0-0	♘e4-d6?

Black unnecessarily moves his knight a third time and makes his first small error. The rules of development demand 7...♘b8-c6 or 7...0-0.

8 ♗c1-f4

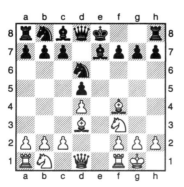

Good aggressive development by White. Black played 7...♘e4-d6 so that he could swap off the bishops by 8...♗c8-f5. Now this would lose a piece to 9 ♗f4xd6.

8 ...   ♘b8-c6
Sensible development...
9 ♖f1-e1   ♘c6-b4?
...but why move the knight a second time? Because Black has a plan! A good plan but at the wrong time ... and he hasn't taken any notice of White's last move!

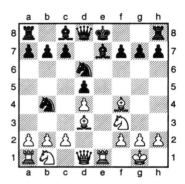

The time lost with 9...♘c6-b4 doesn't matter as White will not want to let the knight capture on d3 so he will lose a move as well with his bishop. But 9...♘c6-b4 signals the beginning of an attack at a time when Black should be developing pieces. It is also careless, as it ignores the power of the rook on the open e-file. 9...0-0 is the sensible move.

10 ♗d3-f1
Black's plan becomes clear. The white bishop avoids exchange...
10 ...   ♗c8-f5
...the black bishop develops aggressively, threatening c2...
11 ♘b1-a3
...and the white knight is forced to a poor square in order to defend.
11 ...   ♘d6-c4?

This is the whole point of Black's plan. He will exchange knights and then capture on c2.

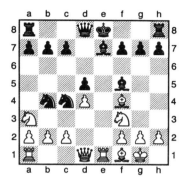

Of course it is wrong to move the knight yet again. Of course it is wrong to try to pinch the c-pawn. Of course it is wrong to start attacking when he is behind in development and his king is still in the centre.

But worse! The plan is wrong because it doesn't even work! It was absolutely essential for Black to castle.

12 ᥒa3xc4   d5xc4
13 ᥕf1xc4!

White just ignores the threat to c2. His bishop finds a splendid diagonal and f7 comes under fire.

13 ...   ᥒb4xc2
14 ᥖe1-e5!

This is what Black had overlooked when he formed his plan four moves ago. If he now captures on a1 he will lose both bishop and knight.

14 ...   ᥕd8-d7
15 ᥖa1-c1   ᥒc2-b4

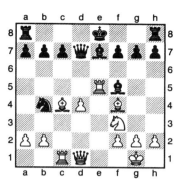

White's last piece has been developed. Both rooks stand on open files, both bishops have good diagonals, the knight is hitting the centre, and the queen is poised for e2 or b3.

Black has three moves to make up.

If he could now magically play ...0-0, ...ᥖf8-e8, and ...ᥖa8-d8 his position would be fine. But he can't. He hasn't castled so his king isn't safe and his rooks are useless.

16 ᥕc4xf7+!!

Crunch! With one simple strike Black's position is blown away.

16 ...   ᥗe8-d8

Both 16...ᥗe8xf7 and 16...ᥗe8-f8 are met by 17 ᥖc1xc7! followed by 18 ᥖe5xf5(+).

17 ᥖe5xe7!   Resigns

Because the black queen is lost after both 17...ᥕd7xe7 18 ᥕf4-g5 and 17...ᥗd8xe7 18 ᥖc1xc7.

The story of this game is spelt out in the note after move 15. Inevitably death came quickly!

Game 10

...in which the white queen becomes a tin-opener.

A. Machulsky v Gurevich
USSR 1976
French Defence

1 e2-e4   e7-e6
2 d2-d4   d7-d5
3 ♘b1-c3   ♘g8-f6
4 ♗c1-g5   ♗f8-b4

An aggressive variation of the French Defence named after the American amateur John McCutcheon, who first played it against World Champion Steinitz in an 1885 simultaneous display.

5 e4-e5   h7-h6
6 ♗g5-d2   ♘f6-d7

This is rather passive. McCutcheon's idea was to play 6...♗b4xc3 and 7...♘f6-e4.

7 ♕d1-g4

Good aggressive development. The black pieces have abandoned the kingside so the white queen targets g7.

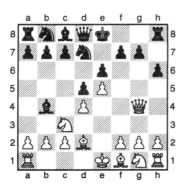

Black immediately has a problem. What to do about his g-pawn? He doesn't like 7...g7-g6 because it leaves a nasty hole on f6. He doesn't like 7...♚e8-f8 as it surrenders the right to castle and leaves the rook looking silly in the corner. So...

7 ...   ♗b4-f8

...he undevelops his bishop! Why? Are the alternatives really so bad?

Well, this is an instructive type of position. Let's consider this line of thinking:

a) The centre pawns are locked together.

b) There is no immediate chance of the pawns being exchanged.

c) There is no immediate chance of lines being opened in the centre.

d) White's pieces will not have the files and diagonals vital for a quick attack.

e) White's lead in development does not matter.

There is some truth in this as a general idea but will it apply to this position?

8 ♘g1-f3

White carries on developing. He could also begin a line-opening plan with 8 f2-f4 hoping to play f4-f5 and exchange on e6. Then he would have a hole on g6 and an open file for his rook.

8 ...   c7-c5

Standard play in French positions. Black challenges White's centre.

9 d4xc5   ♘d7xc5

In view of what is about to happen to him maybe Black should have played 9...♘b8-c6, hitting e5, before regaining the pawn.

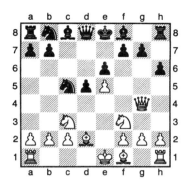

10 b2-b4   ♘c5-d7
11 ♘c3-b5!

Now White's lead in development has become important. The knight is set to land on d6. The bishop on f8 is now overloaded with two squares to defend, so...

11 ...   g7-g6
12 ♗f1-d3

Excellent aggressive development.

12 ...   h6-h5?

Black is worried about an eventual ♗d3xg6, and cracks under the pressure.

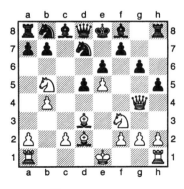

13 ♕g4xe6+!!

Wonderful! The lid is sliced off Black's defences and his king is laid bare.

13 ...   f7xe6

Blocking the check was also hopeless:

a) 13...♗f8-e7 14 ♘b5-d6+ ♚e8-f8 15 ♕e6xf7 is mate.

b) 13...♕d8-e7 14 ♘b5-c7+ costs a rook.

14 ♗d3xg6+

The position has opened up and now White's development matters.

14 ...   ♚e8-e7
15 ♗d2-g5+

White's minor pieces swarm like ants all over the black king.

15 ...   ♘d7-f6
16 e5xf6+!   ♚e7-d7
17 ♘f3-e5 mate

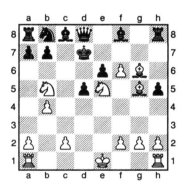

Beautiful!

Game 11

...in which a blundered pawn becomes a brilliant sacrifice.

M. Najdorf v L. Portisch
Varna Olympiad 1962
Queen's Gambit Declined

1	d2-d4	d7-d5
2	c2-c4	e7-e6
3	♘b1-c3	♘g8-f6
4	♘g1-f3	c7-c5
5	c4xd5	♘f6xd5
6	e2-e3	c5xd4

Najdorf was pretty happy when he saw this move because...

7   e3xd4

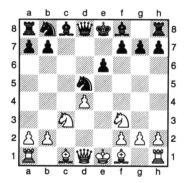

...it opens the diagonal for the white bishop from c1.

7   ...   ♗f8-b4

But when Black played this move without a second's thought Najdorf began to wonder whether he was still happy. He didn't think this variation had ever been played before. It must be something Portisch had worked out before the game and he was beginning

to wonder if there was a catch. Still, he could not see anything wrong with his position so he got on with sensible development.

8	♕d1-c2	♘b8-c6
9	♗f1-d3	♘d5xc3
10	b2xc3	♘c6xd4!?

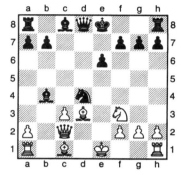

Now White was not at all happy. This was not a move he had seen coming!

11   ♘f3xd4

What else? 11 c3xd4 isn't legal and 11 ♕c2-a4+ ♘d4-c6 12 c3xb4 ♕d8xd3 leaves him a pawn down, unable to castle, and threatened with 13...♕d3-c3+.

11   ...   ♕d8xd4

Any thoughts of happiness had been replaced by total misery in Najdorf's mind. He can't take the queen, he can't take the bishop. He is simply a pawn down. Black must have a winning game!

Yet, as he began to overcome the shock, Najdorf's opening senses began to tell him that everything might not be so bad after all.

12   ♗d3-b5+!

Now Black is forced to give up the right to castle.

12 ... ♔e8-e7

The alternative, 12...♗c8-d7 13 ♗b5xd7+ ♔e8xd7 14 ♕c2-a4+, loses the other bishop.

13 0-0

Najdorf is now able to get on with completing his development whilst Portisch has to untangle his queen and bishop.

13 ... ♕d4xc3

After 13...♗b4xc3 White gets a good diagonal for his bishop by 14 ♗c1-a3+ and then a good file for his rook by 15 ♖a1-d1. Black just gets trouble for his king!

14 ♕c2-e2! ♗b4-d6

Anything on a1 will be loose! 14...♕c3xa1 loses to 15 ♗c1-g5+.

15 ♗c1-b2 ♕c3-a5

Portisch's opening plan has backfired. Winning the pawns put him on a slippery slope and now he can't get off. He can't stop moving his queen and bishop!

16 ♖f1-d1!

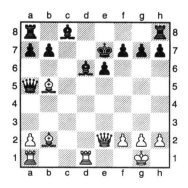

This position tells the story of the game. Black has had to waste a lot of time and he has got his king caught in the centre. This is what Najdorf realized when he had calmed down after move eleven. His basic knowledge of opening play told him that he should be able to mobilize and gain excellent lines for attack. This is exactly what has happened and for Black the end is near.

16 ... ♖h8-d8

White was threatening 17 ♖d1xd6 ♔e7xd6 18 ♕e2-e5+ ♔d6-e7 19 ♕e5-c5+.

17 ♕e2-h5! f7-f6

Black's queen is loose on the rank after 17...♗c8-d7 18 ♕h5-g5+ ♔e7-e8 19 ♗b5xd7+.

18 ♕h5xh7 ♔e7-f7

19 ♗b5-e2!

Threatening 20 ♗e2-h5+ followed by a queen invasion on h8 and g7.

19 ... ♕a5-g5

20 ♗b2-c1 ♗d6xh2+

21 ♔g1xh2 ♕g5-e5+

22 f2-f4 **Resigns**

The game was played on the top board of the match between Argentina and Hungary in the 1962 Olympiad. When it was over many of the competitors congratulated Miguel Najdorf on his 'brilliant pawn sacrifice'. It was only later that he admitted losing the pawn was an accident!

Quite a clever accident really!

Game 12

...in which White is transported back to the Nineteenth Century.

V. Topalov v E. Bareev
Linares 1994
French Defence

1	e2-e4	e7-e6
2	d2-d4	d7-d5
3	♘b1-c3	♘g8-f6
4	♗c1-g5	d5xe4
5	♘c3xe4	♗f8-e7
6	♗g5xf6	♗e7xf6
7	c2-c3	♘b8-d7
8	♕d1-c2	

8 ♘g1-f3 is the normal move in this position and seems to make more sense. Why commit the queen so early? *Always play first the moves you know you will have to make.*

8 ... e6-e5!

Black grabs the chance to fight for space in the centre.

9 d4xe5?

White is dreaming up a very bad plan! 9 0-0-0 e5xd4 10 ♘e4xf6+ ♕d8xf6 11 ♖d1xd4 would have been much better.

9 ... ♘d7xe5

The black knight moves to the centre and clears the path for the bishop on c8.

What can White do now?

10 0-0-0 isn't legal and that wretched black knight controls all the squares he would like to put his pieces: the bishop can't go to d3 or c4 and after 10 ♘g1-f3 ♘e5xf3+ 11 g2xf3 his pawn position is a mess.

10 f2-f4

White solves his immediate problem with force: he kicks the black knight out of the centre. Sadly, this does not help because...

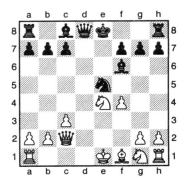

a) The pawn move f2-f4 is not a developing move.

b) The move leaves a nasty hole on e3 and...

10 ... ♘e5-g6

c) ...the pawn comes under immediate attack.

11 g2-g3

Topalov is forced into yet another pawn move and begins to fall behind in development. Worse, this time the pawn move leaves gaping holes on f3 and h3.

11 ... 0-0

Black tucks his king into safety and prepares his rook for action on the open e-file.

12 ♗f1-d3

Ideally 12 ♗f1-g2 would be better as it defends the weak light squares on the kingside. However, White wants to play 0-0-0 and for this he needs first to block the d-file.

12 ... ♕d8-d5!

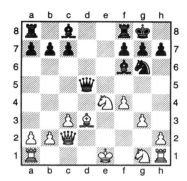

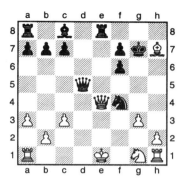

Black instantly homes in on White's weak spots. His queen eyes the loose rook on h1 and attacks a2, preventing 13 0-0-0.

13 a2-a3?

Topalov pursues his plan of castling queenside and makes yet another pawn move. This one proves fatal! He should have tried 13 ♘g1-e2, which at least develops a piece.

13 ... ♘g6xf4!!
14 ♘e4xf6+

White's king is stuck in the centre and he has no control over the light squares on his kingside. If 14 g3xf4 he opens the diagonal from h4 to his king and loses to 14...♗f6-h4+ and 15...f7-f5.

14 ... g7xf6
15 ♗d3xh7+ ♔g8-g7
16 ♕c2-e4

Now the white rook is loose on h1 so there is no time to take the knight. 16 ♗h7-e4 looks to save everything but walks into the usual trouble on the open e-file: 16...♖f8-e8 pins and wins.

16 ... ♖f8-e8!!

17 ♕e4xe8 ♗c8-f5!!

A double rook sacrifice! Topalov must have thought he was back in the nineteenth century when the giants of the game, Anderssen and Morphy, amazed the world with their sacrificial fireworks.

18 ♕e8xa8

Topalov is now two rooks ahead and he would be doing rather nicely if he didn't have a king.

But he has ... and it is about to be mated.

18 ... ♕d5-e4+
19 ♔e1-f2 ♕e4-g2+
20 ♔f2-e3 ♘f4-d5+

Trapped in the centre, caught in the open, his army scattered on the edge, the white king can run but there is nowhere to hide.

21 ♔e3-d4 ♕g2-d2+
22 ♔d4-c5 ♕d2-e3+!
23 ♔c5-c4

Or 23 ♔c5xd5 ♗f5-e6 mate.

23 ... ♘d5-b6+
24 Resigns

Bareev's masterpiece concludes with mate in three moves.

Game 13

...in which Black exchanges pieces and loses all his moves.

O. Duras v St Jes
Pisek 1912
King's Gambit

1	e2-e4	e7-e5
2	f2-f4	e5xf4
3	♘g1-f3	d7-d5
4	e4xd5	♕d8xd5?

This invites White to gain time attacking the queen. 4...♘g8-f6 is normal.

5	♘b1-c3	♕d5-h5
6	d2-d4	♗c8-g4
7	♗c1xf4	♗g4xf3?

Black is behind in development so he doesn't really want to waste more time with another pawn move, but nevertheless 7...c7-c6 is better.

8	♕d1xf3	♕h5xf3
9	g2xf3	

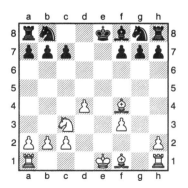

Oldřich Duras was one of the top ten players in the world in 1912. St Jes

was an amateur ... and like many people playing a master he believed that by swapping off the queens he was avoiding danger.

St Jes was wrong!

Just look at the position. Just look at White's big lead in development. What has happened to Black's eight moves?

9	...	♘b8-c6

Again 9...c7-c6 was safer but then White develops another piece.

10	♗f4xc7	♘c6xd4

Now the knight becomes a target.

11	0-0-0	♘d4-e6?

Bad ... but what else can he do?

a) 11...♘d4xf3 12 ♗f1-g2 ♘f3-g5 13 ♗g2xb7 wins a rook.

b) 11...♗f8-c5 12 ♘c3-a4 ♘d4-e6 13 ♘a4xc5 ♘e6xc7 14 ♘c5xb7 is a slow death.

c) 11...♘d4-c6 12 ♗f1-h3 ♘g8-f6 13 ♖h1-e1+ is killing.

12	♗f1-b5+	♔e8-e7
13	♘c3-d5 mate	

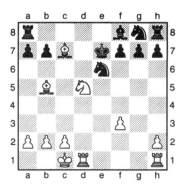

Going out of your way to exchange pieces doesn't avoid danger ... it just wastes time!

Game 14

...in which the rules appear to be wrong.

A. Alekhine v R. Bruce
Plymouth 1938
Caro-Kann Defence

1	e2-e4	c7-c6
2	♘b1-c3	d7-d5
3	♘g1-f3	d5xe4
4	♘c3xe4	♗c8-f5?

Life can be tough! Poor Black. He follows the rules, he develops a piece, he develops aggressively attacking the knight ... and he makes a mistake. Let's see why:

5 ♘e4-g3

White in his turn gains time; the black bishop must move again.

5 ...   ♗f5-g6?

It is always difficult admitting you have made a mistake! g4 was the correct square for the bishop but if Black puts it there now he feels a bit silly for not putting it there last move. Rather than look silly he makes a worse move!

6 h2-h4!

And what's this? A pawn move, on the edge of the board which doesn't help with development? Surely a mistake? No, the h-pawn simply highlights Black's error. It threatens to advance one more square and trap the bishop.

6 ...   h7-h6

Black digs an escape hole on h7.

7 ♘f3-e5!

Now White unnecessarily moves his knight a second time. Surely this must be another mistake? Again no. White threatens 8 ♘e5xg6 f7xg6 with ♕d1-g4 and ♗f1-d3 to follow. The knight has taken up a fine central position and Black loses time moving his bishop yet again.

7 ...   ♗g6-h7
8 ♕d1-h5

Aggressive development targeting f7. Black has only one move...

8 ...   g7-g6

...and buries his bishop alive!

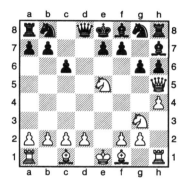

9 ♗f1-c4!!   e7-e6

It is mate if he takes the queen.

10 ♕h5-e2   ♘g8-f6?

Again a logical developing move is a mistake! It is not enough just to *follow* the rules. You have to calculate the moves as well, just to make sure they work.

11 ♘e5xf7!

Forking queen and rook.

11 ...   ♔e8xf7
12 ♕e2xe6+   Resigns

Since 12...♔f7-g7 13 ♕e6-f7 is mate.

When White appeared to break the rules he didn't lose time ... he gained it!

Game 15

...in which the board belongs to White.

A. Nimzowitsch v S. Alapin
Riga 1913
French Defence

1	e2-e4	e7-e6
2	d2-d4	d7-d5
3	♘b1-c3	♘g8-f6
4	e4xd5	♘f6xd5

Planting a knight in the centre of the board cannot be bad but this is still a strange decision. By recapturing with the pawn, Black would have controlled the central squares e4 and c4 and he would have opened the diagonal for his bishop from c8.

5	♘g1-f3	c7-c5
6	♘c3xd5	♕d8xd5

Again 6...e6xd5 would be more sensible.

7	♗c1-e3	c5xd4
8	♘f3xd4	a7-a6

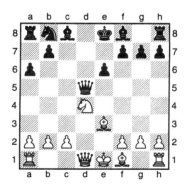

Black didn't really want to play a pawn move and he didn't want to leave a hole on b6 but he had to stop 9 ♘d4-b5.

9 ♗f1-e2! ♕d5xg2?

An amazing move from a player with over thirty years of top international experience behind him! Every instinct must have told Simon Alapin that White's forces would now seize control of the board. 9...♗f8-e7 still leaves him behind in development but gives him some hope of putting up a fight.

10 ♗e2-f3

Naturally the bishop accepts the fine diagonal...

10 ... ♕g2-g6

...and the queen has to move yet again.

11 ♕d1-d2

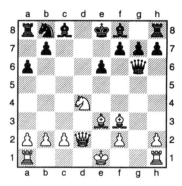

White has four pieces in play, Black only one. Worse still for Black, it isn't easy for him to get his pieces into the game. He can't allow either 11...♘b8-c6 12 ♘d4xc6 or 11...♗c8-d7 12 ♗f3xb7.

11 ... e6-e5

Maybe this was the move Alapin was relying upon when he played 10...♕d5xg2. At first sight it seems to solve a lot of his problems as it has three very good points in its favour:

a) it kicks the white knight back and out of the centre.

b) it threatens 12...e5-e4 driving the white bishop away.

c) it opens the diagonal for the c8-bishop to develop.

Yes, 11...e6-e5 has three very good points in its favour. Sadly for Alapin none of them matter.

12 0-0-0!!

Now that White has so many open lines and such active pieces he must seize the initiative.

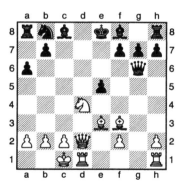

There is an immediate threat of 13 ♘d4-e6 followed by either 14 ♕d2-d8 mate or 14 ♘e6-c7+ so Black has to capture.

12 ...   e5xd4

13 ♗e3xd4

White has full control of the centre; his pieces co-ordinate to breathe fire in all directions.

13 ...   ♘b8-c6

Now White has several ways of winning. The most obvious is 14 ♗f3xc6+ ♕g6xc6 15 ♗d4xg7 threatening both

the rook and 16 ♕d2-d8 mate but Nimzowitsch pulls out something really special.

14 ♗d4-f6!!

This has the threat of 15 ♕d2-d8+ ♘c6xd8 16 ♖d1xd8 mate.

14 ...   ♕g6xf6

White controls the board and Black has nothing better. Against 14...g7xf6, 14...♗f8-e7 or 14...♗c8-e6 White simply plays 15 ♗f3xc6+ and 16 ♕d2-d8+ mating.

15 ♖h1-e1+

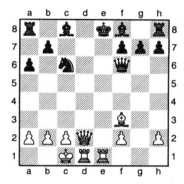

Take a long hard look at this diagram and make sure its message is fixed firmly in your mind! The white king is safe behind a pawn shield. The white rooks have come to power together down the open files. The black rooks are useless. Black's king is about to die. The message: *Get Castled!*

15 ...   ♗f8-e7

Or 15...♗c8-e6 16 ♕d2-d7 mate.

16 ♗f3xc6+   ♔e8-f8

Or 16...b7xc6 17 ♕d2-d8 mate.

17 ♕d2-d8+!!   ♗e7xd8

18 ♖e1-e8 mate

All power to the rooks.

Game 16

...in which the black queen suffers from her husband's lack of air.

W.T. Bradford v J.C. Dyson
Liverpool 1964
Sicilian Defence

1	e2-e4	c7-c5
2	♘g1-f3	♘b8-c6
3	♗f1-c4	d7-d6
4	0-0	♘g8-f6
5	♖f1-e1	♗c8-g4
6	c2-c3	♘c6-e5?

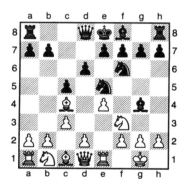

Black has a plan! But as we might expect from a plan which begins by moving a piece for a second time on move six, it is not a very good plan! 6...e7-e6 is much better.

     7   ♗c4-b5+
7 ♘f3xe5 forces 7...d6xe5.

     7 ...   ♘f6-d7??
7...♘e5-d7 isn't too bad for Black.

Black concentrates on his plan. He is dreaming of 8...♘e5xf3+ 9 g2xf3 ♗g4-h3 when White's king is opened up, the black queen will rush into the attack, and, he hopes, mate will follow quickly.

Wonderful!

He thinks that White can only prevent this by the miserable retreat 8 ♗b5-e2.

He's wrong!

Black has now moved both of his knights twice and, as so often happens when the rules are broken, he is punished by an immediate tactical trick:

     8   ♘f3xe5!!

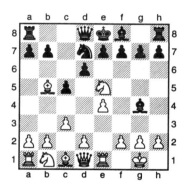

You can see in the previous diagram that when Black began his plan, his g4-bishop was defended by both knights. Now it is loose. Of course he can take the white queen...

     8 ...   ♗g4xd1
...but his king has no breathing space and after...

     9   ♗b5xd7+
...he has to give up his own queen...

     9 ...   ♕d8xd7
...but still loses a piece...

     10   ♘e5xd7   Resigns
After 10...♗d1-g4 11 ♘d7xf8 or 10...♔e8xd7 11 ♖e1xd1 he is a man short.

Game 17

...in which Black shows his artistic talent ... and White shows his appreciation.

J. Hector v J. Vidarsson
Reykjavik 1996
Sicilian Defence

1	e2-e4	c7-c5
2	♘g1-f3	e7-e6
3	d2-d4	c5xd4
4	♘f3xd4	a7-a6

When the Russian master Ilia Kan developed this system of the Sicilian he knew he was making a lot of pawn moves, he knew he was leaving holes on the dark squares d6 and b6 and he knew he would have to develop his pieces quickly to avoid trouble.

| 5 | ♘b1-c3 | g7-g6?! |

Vidarsson is playing with fire! He arranges *all* his pawns in an artistic pattern on the light squares. Very pretty! But now there are holes on b6, d6, f6 and h6, which his dark-squared bishop will have problems defending.

| 6 | ♗c1-e3! |

Hector immediately seizes on the weaknesses! He races his dark-squared bishop into action.

| 6 | ... | ♗f8-g7 |
| 7 | ♘d4-b3 |

This knight hits a5 and c5 and clears the path of the e3-bishop. The other white knight is about to leap into a4 and increase the pressure on the dark squares.

| 7 | ... | ♘g8-e7? |

Black would love to get rid of the knight on c3 but with all his pawns on light squares the last thing he wants to do is swap his dark-squared bishop. He doesn't like 7...♘g8-f6 blocking the bishop's diagonal either so he puts the knight on e7 ... and loses immediately! He had to play 7...b7-b5.

| 8 | ♘c3-a4! |

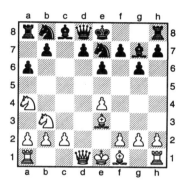

Hector appreciates a pretty picture when he sees one ... and this is it! All the important dark squares are on the queenside, far away from Black's bishop, and Hector exploits them perfectly. Vidarsson spots that 9 ♘a4-b6 ♖a8-a7 10 ♘b6xc8 is threatened so he saves his rook and...

| 8 | ... | ♘b8-c6 |
| 9 | ♗e3-b6 |

...loses his queen instead!

| 9 | ... | **Resigns** |

As a rough rule in the opening you should try to share your pawns between the dark and light squares. Poor Vidarsson put all his on light squares and the game was played on the dark ones.

Game 18

...in which White is cut in two and his forces become strangers to each other.

E. Eliskases v L. Steiner
Budapest 1933
English Opening

1	c2-c4	♘g8-f6
2	♘b1-c3	e7-e5
3	♘g1-f3	♘b8-c6
4	e2-e3	♗f8-b4
5	♘c3-d5?	

White sets off on a time-wasting manoeuvre. The natural move was 5 ♕d1-c2 in order to control e4 and to be able to recapture if necessary on c3 with the queen.

5	...	e5-e4!
6	♘d5xb4	♘c6xb4
7	♘f3-d4	0-0

White's opening has been a total failure. He has created a nasty hole on d3 and spent three moves exchanging his knight for a bishop. Black has just let White get on with it! He has built a lead in development and accepted the invitation for his knight to attack the hole.

8 ♗f1-e2?

The immediate 8 a2-a3 was better. White is not aware that danger is building up on d3.

8 ... d7-d5!

Black plants a pawn in the centre and seizes more space.

9 a2-a3? ♘b4-d3+!

A nasty shock for White, who expected the knight to retreat.

10 ♗e2xd3

Virtually forced since the alternative 10 ♔e1-f1 leaves the knight triumphant and White with great problems as to how to complete his development.

10 ... e4xd3

White probably thought the d3-pawn would be weak and that he could simply attack it and win it. It isn't! He can't! It simply cuts him in two.

11 c4-c5

After 11 c4xd5 ♕d8xd5 the black queen claims the centre and White's kingside comes under fire.

11 ... ♘f6-e4!

Black realizes that for him the opening is near its end and it is time for action. His knight seizes a fine central square: he attacks f2 and he forces White to defend the c5-pawn.

12 b2-b4

White has to defend. Having fallen behind in development he has to answer Black's threats. He just can't find time to develop his pieces.

12 ... ♕d8-g5!

Black has seized the initiative. With better development and control of the centre, his pieces develop naturally with threats.

13 g2-g3

White grovels to defend g2 and makes new holes on h3 and f3. However, 13 0-0 ♗c8-g4 14 f2-f3 ♗g4-h3 is just awful.

13 ... ♗c8-h3!

The bishop leaps into the hole, seizes control of f1 and prevents White from castling.

14 f2-f3

White thinks it's time to evict the knight from e4. The only trouble is...

14 ... f7-f5!!

...the knight won't go!

15 ♕d1-b3

Too late White realizes that after 15 f3xe4 f5xe4 the black queen skips from g5 to f6 and mates on the f-file.

15 ... f5-f4!!

White's forces make a pathetic sight. They stand like strangers, uncoordinated and unaware of each other's existence. Worse, the d3-pawn cuts

White's position in two, trapping his king in the centre. Black's forces are ready for action so he smashes open the files for his rooks.

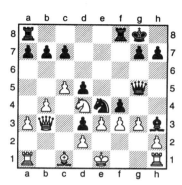

16 e3xf4

Everything else loses:

a) 16 g3xf4 ♕g5-g2 with unavoidable mate.

b) 16 f3xe4 f4xg3 rips his kingside apart.

16 ... ♖a8-e8!!

Side by side the rooks dominate the central files.

17 f4xg5 ♘e4xc5+
18 ♔e1-d1 ♘c5xb3

Black wins back the queen but he is after much more ... *checkmate!*

19 ♘d4xb3 ♗h3-g2

The bishop 'forks' rook and mate.

20 ♘b3-d4 ♗g2xh1
21 f3-f4 ♖e8-e4!
22 ♗c1-b2 ♖f8-e8
23 Resigns

The d3-pawn is stuck in White's throat and it is mate on e1.

Game 19

...in which White strikes whilst the iron is hot.

R. Spielmann v H. Wahle
Vienna 1926
French Defence

1	e2-e4	e7-e6
2	d2-d4	d7-d5
3	♘b1-c3	♘g8-f6
4	e4xd5	e6xd5
5	♗c1-g5	♗f8-e7
6	♗f1-d3	♘b8-c6
7	♘g1-e2	

Because White had the first move he has been able to develop a little more aggressively. His dark-squared bishop pinned the black knight and Black replied defensively with ...♗f8-e7. His light-squared bishop has taken a fine diagonal and h7 will be its target when Black castles. The black light-squared bishop cannot use f5 for a base. Indeed f5 is the square to which the white knight is now heading.

7 ... ♘c6-b4?

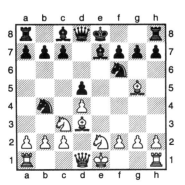

Eliskases made this mistake in our last game! Wahle doesn't like the look of the d3-bishop so he sets out to exchange it. But of course...

8	♘e2-g3	♘b4xd3+
9	♕d1xd3	

...the black knight made three moves, the white bishop only one, so White has gained a lead in development.

9 ... g7-g6?

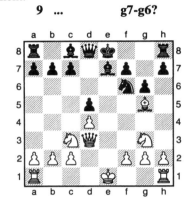

Sometimes the medicine causes more discomfort than the pain it was sent to cure! There are a lot of open lines on the board and Black expects that his bishops will be better than White's knights. He desperately wants to avoid exchanging them so he prevents 10 ♘g3-f5. However, after 9...g7-g6 he has permanent holes on f6 and h6 and he would have done much better with 9...0-0.

10 0-0 c7-c6

This protects the d-pawn and opens a diagonal for the queen. Normally this would be a good idea but it is another pawn move and Black is already behind in development.

11 ♖a1-e1 0-0

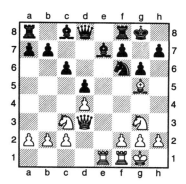

White's army is at action stations whilst Black is a full three moves behind. White must strike whilst the iron is hot! Black must not be given time to sort out his muddle.

12 &Re1xe7!!

Splat!

12 ...   &Wd8xe7

13 &Wd3-f3

White seized his chance at just the right moment, when his forces were prepared and Black's were not.

White gave up his rook to:

a) get rid of Black's bishop, which was defending the dark squares.

b) use those dark squares for his own attack.

c) trap the black knight in a murderous pin.

Black will now be too busy defending to complete his development.

13 ...   &Kg8-g7

The alternative was 13...&c8-f5 14 &Ng3xf5 g6xf5 15 &Wf3-g3 when death follows quickly on the dark squares.

14 &Nc3-e4!

All White's efforts are now aimed at hammering the nail home on f6.

14 ...   d5xe4

15 &Ng3xe4

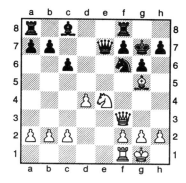

The power of the pin ... there is no escape for the black knight. Worse! There is no escape for the black king either.

15 ...   &We7-e6

Or 15...&We7xe4 16 &Wf3xf6+ &Kg7-g8 17 &g5-h6.

Either way Black just has no control over the dark squares.

16 &g5xf6+   &Kg7-g8

17 &Wf3-f4   Resigns

After 18 &Wf4-h6 the white queen and bishop will stand triumphant in the two holes and mate will follow on g7.

Maybe Black should not have played 9...g7-g6! The trouble with pawns is that they can never go back to cover the weak squares they have left behind them.

Game 20

...in which the supported queen accomplishes what the lone queen cannot.

Judge A. Meek v P. Morphy
Mobile 1855
Scotch Gambit

1	e2-e4	e7-e5
2	♘g1-f3	♘b8-c6
3	d2-d4	e5xd4
4	♗f1-c4	♗f8-c5
5	♘f3-g5?	

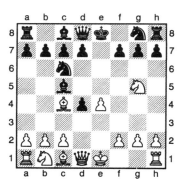

The American genius Paul Morphy was by far the strongest player of the nineteenth century and one of the strongest of all time. He was eighteen and already a young star when he played this game, and so for Meek to imagine that he was going to bowl Morphy over with a crude attack on f7 was more than a little optimistic!

In moving the knight for a second time Meek moves it away from the battle to control the centre.

    5   ...   ♘g8-h6!

Black's knight has to move to a poor square on the very edge of the board in order to defend ... but at least it develops!

6	♘g5xf7	♘h6xf7
7	♗c4xf7+	♔e8xf7
8	♕d1-h5+	g7-g6
9	♕h5xc5	d7-d6

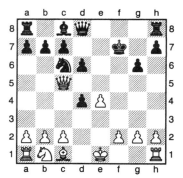

Meek's plan has gone horribly wrong. He has opened up the black king and if he had a lead in development he could hope to launch an early attack. But he hasn't! In opening up the king he has had to exchange the only two minor pieces he had managed to develop. Now he has only his queen in play and...

    10 ♕c5-b5

...as so often happens when the queen is left unsupported, she has to run for her life.

    10 ...   ♖h8-e8

Morphy seizes the initiative!

    11 ♕b5-b3+   d6-d5!

Morphy blocks the check and hits the e-pawn a second time. Now 12 ♕b3xd5+? blunders the queen, therefore...

    12 f2-f3

...White props up his e-pawn but opens the h4-diagonal to his king in doing so.

12 ... ♘c6-a5!

Rooks need open files! Morphy wants to get at the white king. He wants to play ...d5xe4 so he needs to unpin his d-pawn.

However, 12...♘c6-a5 looks a strange way of doing it. It puts the knight on the edge of the board and the d-pawn could have been unpinned by 12...♔f7-g7. True, but time is important! Furthermore Morphy knows that his own king is in the open and will be in danger if Meek is able to develop quickly. After 12...♔f7-g7 13 0-0! White's pieces race into action and Black dare not risk 13...d5xe4 14 f3xe4 ♖e8xe4 15 ♕b3-f7+ ♔g7-h8 16 ♗c1-h6. With 12...♘c6-a5 he attacks the queen and denies White the luxury of castling.

13 ♕b3-d3 d5xe4
14 f3xe4 ♕d8-h4+

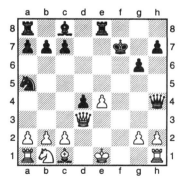

Now it is the white king who is threatened and he really is in danger because...

15 g2-g3 ♖e8xe4+

...the black queen has support!

16 ♔e1-f2 ♕h4-e7
17 ♘b1-d2

White develops ... and with a threat! But it is all too late.

17 ... ♖e4-e3
18 ♕d3-b5

Or 18 ♕d3xd4 ♖e3-e2+ 19 ♔f2-f3 ♗c8-h3!.

18 ... c7-c6
19 ♕b5-f1 ♗c8-h3!

Morphy's pieces are going to war! If the bishop is taken, 20...♖e3-e2+ quickly leads to mate.

20 ♕f1-d1 ♖a8-f8!

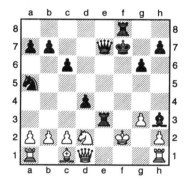

Morphy finds an excellent open file for his rook and completes his development. Apart from the knight, which has already done its job, his pieces coordinate perfectly.

21 ♘d2-f3 ♔f7-e8!
22 Resigns

Since 22 ♗c1xe3 ♕e7xe3 is mate and otherwise he collapses on f3.

Don't attack unless your pieces are able to give support!

Game 21

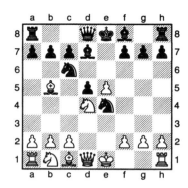

...in which the queens fight it out and victory goes to the lady with armed support.

T. Lichtenhein v P. Morphy
New York 1857
Two Knights Defence

1	e2-e4	e7-e5
2	♘g1-f3	♘b8-c6
3	d2-d4	e5xd4
4	♗f1-c4	♘g8-f6

The knight develops aggressively, attacking the white e-pawn...

5 e4-e5

...which responds by attacking the black knight! Now, where should the knight go? To e4 or to g4?

5 ... d7-d5!

Neither! Both knight moves are all right but Morphy understands the importance of the centre and of speedy development in this open position. With 5...d7-d5 he attacks the white bishop and the central square e4 and he opens the line for his light-squared bishop.

6 ♗c4-b5

White doesn't have much choice as after 6 e5xf6 d5xc4 7 f6xg7 ♗f8xg7 he isn't going to get his pawn back.

6 ... ♘f6-e4

The d5-pawn now supports the black knight.

7 ♘f3xd4

White regains his pawn and has the threat of 8 ♘d4xc6 winning the exchange and a pawn.

7 ... ♗c8-d7

Black can be quite happy with his opening. He has countered White's threats, he has a strong pawn in the centre and he has three pieces in play to White's two.

8 ♘d4xc6

8 ♗b5xc6 is usually played here but as we shall see White has a plan!

8 ... b7xc6
9 ♗b5-d3 ♗f8-c5!

Morphy has a plan as well! He continues to develop aggressively and hits the target square f2.

10 ♗d3xe4

White's plan is to win in the endgame. He sees that 10...d5xe4 leaves Black's pawn position in a mess. He believes the pawn on e4 will be easy to attack and he sees that the doubled and isolated pawns on c7 and c6 will also be weak.

10 ... ♕d8-h4!

Morphy's plan is to make sure the game never reaches the ending!

11 ♕d1-e2 d5xe4
12 ♗c1-e3?

This looks sensible: it develops a piece and challenges Morphy's bishop on the diagonal to f2.

However, when you are behind in development and your opponent's pieces are aggressively placed on open lines, the safety of your king must come first. Here White should have castled.

12 ...   &d7-g4!

Morphy pursues his plan: White must not be given time to develop.

13 ♕e2-c4

White daren't play 13 ♕e2-d2 ♖a8-d8 so the queen finds safety on c4 and begins a counter-attack. The queen hits the bishop and behind it the pawn on c6 with a threat to fork king and rook.

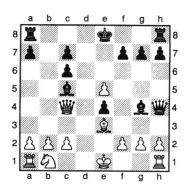

13 ...   &c5xe3!

The board is in flames! Both queens have powerful threats but Morphy will triumph because, just as in his game with Meek, his lady has the support of other forces.

14 g2-g3

Alternatively 14 ♕c4xc6+ &g4-d7 15 ♕c6xa8+ when the main line is 15...&e8-e7 16 g2-g3 &e3xf2+ 17

&e1xf2 e4-e3+ 18 &f2-e1 ♕h4-b4+ 19 c2-c3 ♕b4xb2 20 ♕a8xh8 &d7-g4. Now the white queen has won both rooks on her own but the black queen will win the game because, with bishop and pawn support, she can force mate.

14 ...   ♕h4-d8

Morphy's pieces are so well coordinated that he can retreat and actually threaten mate on d1. Now we can see why White should have castled on move 12.

15 f2xe3   ♕d8-d1+
16 &e1-f2   ♕d1-f3+
17 &f2-g1   &g4-h3

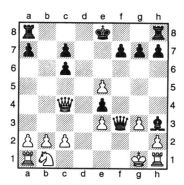

It is now the turn of the white queen to have a little fun but...

18 ♕c4xc6+   &e8-f8!
19 ♕c6xa8+   &f8-e7

...on her own she can only win rooks; she cannot force mate.

20 Resigns

The black lady can! She has the support of her bishop and the pleasant choice between mating on g2 or e3.

Game 22

...in which breaking the rules is playing with fire.

R.G. Record v L. Watson
Oxford 1966
Centre Counter Defence

1 e2-e4	d7-d5
2 e4xd5	♕d8xd5
3 ♘b1-c3	♕d5-a5

This line of the Centre Counter has been used by many top masters yet it breaks the rules of opening play. In three moves Black has allowed his queen to become a target and has committed her for no obvious reason to the edge of the board. However, despite breaking the rules Black has not fallen behind in development and there are no weak points in his position. White can play d2-d4 and gain a small space advantage in the centre ... but that is all ... so long as Black plays with extreme care...

4 ♘g1-f3	♗c8-g4
5 h2-h3	♗g4xf3?

...but he doesn't! Amazingly this casual exchange is close to being a losing move. 5...♗g4-h5 was necessary.

6 ♕d1xf3

The results of Black's carelessness are plain to see. The bishop which made two moves has disappeared for a knight which made only one and the white queen has taken up a beautiful post from which she rakes the diagonal to b7 and a8.

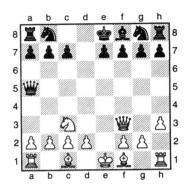

6 ...	♘b8-c6?

Black seems to have no sense of danger. He makes the obvious move and now he is lost. But what else? If 6...♘b8-d7 White can happily pinch the pawn on b7 without falling behind in development. If 6...c7-c6 White will gain a massive position by simple development: 7 ♗f1-c4 e7-e6 and 8 0-0.

7 ♗f1-b5

Threatening to win a rook by capturing twice on c6.

7 ...	♕a5-b6

The black queen is loose on a5, and so 7...♔e8-d7 8 ♕f3-d5+ ♔d7-c8 9 ♗b5xc6 ♕a5xd5 10 ♗c6xd5 loses a piece.

8 ♘c3-d5!

Hitting both the queen and the pawn on c7.

8 ...	♕b6-a5
9 b2-b4	**Resigns**

As 9...♕a5xb5 10 ♘d5xc7+ forks the whole family.

If you play with fire, it is easy to get burnt!

Game 23

...in which White sees the trap but falls into it anyway!

Veitch v J. Penrose
Buxton 1950
Catalan System

1	d2-d4	♘g8-f6
2	c2-c4	e7-e6
3	♘g1-f3	d7-d5
4	g2-g3	d5xc4
5	♘b1-d2	

d2 is not a good square for the knight: it blocks both queen and bishop. However, the knight shouldn't be in the way for long as White plans ♘d2xc4.

5	...	c7-c5
6	d4xc5?	

Dreadful. White swaps his strong centre pawn and helps Black to develop. He should continue as planned with 6 ♘d2xc4 to regain his pawn and unclutter his position.

| 6 | ... | ♗f8xc5 |

The bishop says thank you very much, recaptures and eyes f2.

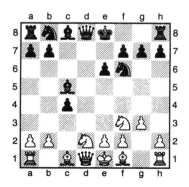

White now has to be careful. He spots the well-known trap and avoids 7 ♘d2xc4 ♗c5xf2+! which would cost him his queen. He relaxes and instead...

| 7 | ♗f1-g2?? | |

...walks smack into another variation of the same tactical theme!

| 7 | ... | ♗c5xf2+!! |
| 8 | ♔e1xf2 | |

8 ♔e1-f1 ♘f6-g4 9 ♕d1-a4+ ♗c8-d7 10 ♕a4xc4 ♘g4-e3+ is just as bad.

| 8 | ... | ♘f6-g4+ |

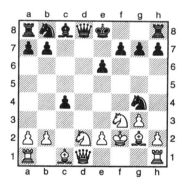

| 9 | ♔f2-e1 | |

This is White's only hope since 9 ♔f2-g1 ♕d8-b6+ mates and 9 ♔f2-f1 ♘g4-e3+ costs him his queen.

| 9 | ... | ♘g4-e3 |
| 10 | **Resigns** | |

After 10 ♕d1-a4+ ♗c8-d7 White only has a3 and b4 for his queen. Take your pick, white queen! On both squares you are forked by 11...♘e3-c2+.

Veitch made a common mistake. He concentrated his energies on avoiding one trap... and walked straight into another one.

Game 24

...in which open lines are more valuable than pawns.

G. Vescovi v I. Sokolov
Malmö 1995
Portuguese Opening

1 e2-e4   e7-e5
2 ♗f1-b5

This move is not to be recommended! The white bishop hits thin air. Now Black has his first decision to make and he plumps for aggression.

2 ...   c7-c6

c6 is the ideal square for the black knight, so why put a pawn there? Well, Black has three aims:

a) He gains time by attacking the white bishop.

b) He opens the diagonal to a5 for his queen.

c) He prepares to support the central advance ...d7-d5.

3 ♗b5-a4   ♘g8-f6

Simple aggressive development.

The knight comes to its best square and hits White's e-pawn.

4 ♕d1-e2   ♗f8-c5
5 ♘g1-f3

As he assessed this unusual position Sokolov was struck by three tactical thoughts:

a) If the e-file could be opened the white king and queen would be in trouble.

b) If White could be encouraged to play ♘f3xe5 it would help to open the file and also put the knight in danger.

c) With his bishop on c5 coordinating with his knight on f6 there will be chances of a sacrifice on f2.

Armed with these thoughts Sokolov found a simple plan screaming at him: Open the lines! Get rid of the pawns!

5 ...   d7-d5!

6 e4xd5

Vescovi is just sucked in to Black's plans. The a4-bishop is loose so 6 d2-d3 ♕d8-a5+ 7 ♘b1-c3 d5-d4 is out of the question.

6 ...   0-0!

The e5-pawn does not matter. Black has one priority: get that rook to e8.

7 ♘f3xe5

Oh dear! Poor Vescovi. He didn't want to take that pawn. He didn't want to open the e-file for Black's rook. But Black was threatening 7...e5-e4 when it is difficult to find a good home for the knight and Black's pieces will walk all over him.

7 ... ♖f8-e8

Two pawns down but aim achieved!

8 c2-c3

After 8 0-0 ♗c5-d4 the knight is lost. Now, however, White has the possibility of solving some of his problems with d2-d4 hitting the black bishop and supporting his knight. What can Black do?

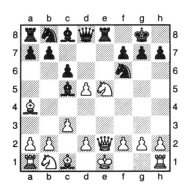

8 ... ♗c5xf2+!

It is not surprising that Black has a tactical trick in this position. His pieces are so well co-ordinated. His rook and knight are already dangerous and his queen and c8-bishop lurk in the background.

9 ♔e1-f1

This looks like surrender but everything is bad for White:

a) 9 ♔e1xf2 ♖e8xe5! 10 ♕e2xe5 allows 10...♘f6-g4+ forking his king and queen.

b) 9 ♕e2xf2 ♖e8xe5+ 10 ♔e1-d1 ♗c8-g4+ 11 ♔d1-c2 ♕d8xd5 and the attack crashes on.

c) 9 ♔e1-d1 ♗c8-g4 wins material.

9 ... ♗c8-g4!

As is so often the case when a player has better development and co-ordination, Sokolov's other pieces develop with threats.

10 ♕e2xf2 ♖e8xe5

A capture, a central post for the rook, and a threat: ...♖e5-f5.

11 ♔f1-g1 ♕d8-e7!

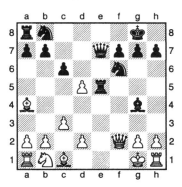

12 Resigns

Black threatens 12...♖e5-e1+ and 12 h2-h3 ♗g4xh3 13 ♖h1xh3 ♖e5-e1+ 14 ♔g1-h2 ♘f6-g4+ costs White his queen.

This was not a risky opening gambit. Sokolov knew exactly what he was getting for his two pawns. Open lines! And he could see how he was going to use them.

Game 25

...in which an extra move allows White to improve on history.

First the history.
One of the most spectacular games ever played was between C. Hamppe and P. Meitner in Vienna in 1872:

1	e2-e4	e7-e5
2	♘b1-c3	♗f8-c5
3	♘c3-a4	♗c5xf2+!?
4	♔e1xf2	♕d8-h4+
5	♔f2-e3	♕h4-f4+
6	♔e3-d3	d7-d5

This threatens mate in two by 7...♕f4xe4+ 8 ♔d3-c3 ♕e4-c4.

7 ♔d3-c3

7 ♕d1-e1 is considered a better try for advantage.

7 ... ♕f4xe4
8 ♔c3-b3

The knight has to be saved and 8 ♘a4-c5 ♕e4-d4+ doesn't help whilst 8 b2-b3 ♕e4-d4 mate is definitely not recommended.

8 ... ♘b8-a6

The threat now is to mate on b4.

9 a2-a3

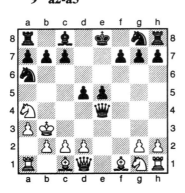

9 ... ♕e4xa4+!!

Only one thing matters in a king-hunt. You must hustle and bustle and harry and chase and worry that king. Never give him a moment's peace, never give him a second to rest and find a safe home. Here Black has run out of checks and against a developing move such as 9...♗c8-d7 White will play 10 ♘a4-c3, tuck his king away on a2 and enjoy life with an extra piece.

10	♔b3xa4	♘a6-c5+
11	♔a4-b4	a7-a5+!
12	♔b4xc5	♘g8-e7

The white king has been imprisoned by the black pawns. 13...b7-b6+ 14 ♔c5-b5 ♗c8-d7 mate is a delightful threat.

White finds the only defence:

13	♗f1-b5+!	♔e8-d8
14	♗b5-c6!	b7-b6+!
15	♔c5-b5	♘e7xc6

Threatening 16...♘c6-d4+ 17 ♔b5-a4 ♗c8-d7 mate.

16 ♔b5xc6

Neither 16 d2-d4 nor 16 c2-c3 stops the knight check on d4 followed by 17...♗c8-d7 mate.

16 ... ♗c8-b7+!!

Amazing! The white king cannot escape from jail and Black can't force checkmate.

17 ♔c6-b5

It is mate if 17 ♔c6xb7 ♚d8-d7 18 ♕d1-g4+ ♚d7-d6 since White can't stop 19...♖h8-b8.

17 ... ♗b7-a6+
18 ♔b5-c6

After 18 ♔b5-a4 ♗a6-c4! White cannot prevent 19...b6-b5 mate.

18 ... ♗a6-b7+

And now since the white king cannot escape the checks and since Black has run out of pieces to sacrifice the players agreed the game **drawn**.

So much for history. Now back to 1989 and our real game:

Schelkonogov v Morozenko
Krasny Luch 1989
Vienna Game

1	e2-e4	e7-e5
2	♘b1-c3	♘b8-c6
3	♗f1-c4	♘c6-a5????

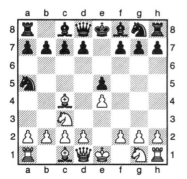

One move ... four mistakes!

Black commits four crimes:

a) He unnecessarily moves his knight a second time.

b) He puts it on a poor square on the edge of the board.

c) He leaves the knight loose.

d) He forgets his history!

4	♗c4xf7+	♔e8xf7
5	♕d1-h5+	♔f7-e6
6	♕h5-f5+	♔e6-d6
7	d2-d4	

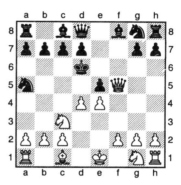

Have you seen this position before? Not exactly. When Meitner reached this position he was Black and didn't have the luxury of a knight already in play.

7 ... ♘a5-c6

The c3-knight makes all the difference as everything now loses for Black. You can improve your tactics and spend a happy hour working all the variations out for yourself!

8	d4xe5+	♔d6-c5
9	♗c1-e3+	♔c5-b4
10	a2-a3+	♔b4-a5
11	e5-e6+	d7-d5
12	e4xd5	♘c6-e7
13	b2-b4+	**Resigns**

Game 26

...in which ...b7-b5 is one pawn move too many.

A. Hall v I. Stern
Zagreb 1957
Sicilian Defence

1	e2-e4	c7-c5
2	♘g1-f3	d7-d6
3	d2-d4	c5xd4
4	♘f3xd4	♘g8-f6
5	♘b1-c3	a7-a6
6	♗c1-g5	♘b8-d7

This looks logical as the knight supports his partner on f6 and may later find a good base on c5 or e5. However, this is still the opening and on d7 the knight rather gets in the way.

7	♗f1-c4	e7-e6
8	0-0	b7-b5?

Black follows a normal Sicilian plan. He advances on the queenside and puts the white e-pawn under pressure: he can play ...♗c8-b7 and he threatens ...b5-b4 kicking the c3-knight away. However...

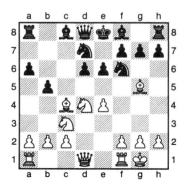

White has developed all his minor pieces and castled. Black has only his knights in play. The last thing Black can afford is another pawn move. Especially a pawn move which opens a diagonal and leaves his rook loose in the corner.

What should White do? It would be sensible to mobilize his queen and rooks *but* with his big lead in development he might expect something better. He should look for an immediate combination.

9 ♗c4xe6!!

Not surprisingly he finds one. Black's defences are ripped apart.

9 ...   f7xe6
10 ♘d4xe6

White has gained a second pawn for his bishop and the black queen is attacked.

10 ...   ♕d8-b6
11 ♘c3-d5

White's pieces are so well placed they just race into the ruins of Black's position. Again the queen is threatened but now there is the added danger of a knight fork on c7.

11 ...   ♘f6xd5
12 ♕d1xd5

Her Majesty enters the field of battle and hits the loose rook ... but the black king is her real target!

12 ...   ♖a8-a7

All methods of saving the rook meet the same answer...

13 ♘e6-c7+! Resigns

Mate with 14 ♕d5-e6+ comes next.

Game 27

...in which Black abandons the centre and his queen is caught in bed.

I. Kondratov v V. Vasiliev
Rostov 1989
Sicilian Defence

1	e2-e4	c7-c5
2	♘g1-f3	♘b8-c6
3	d2-d4	c5xd4
4	♘f3xd4	g7-g6
5	♘b1-c3	♗f8-g7
6	♗c1-e3	♘g8-f6

Normally Black has put a pawn on d6 by now, giving himself a foothold in the centre. He then has hopes of being able to challenge for space forcefully with ...d6-d5 later on. In this Accelerated Dragon Variation Black hopes to save a move and play ...d7-d5 all in one go.

7	♗f1-c4	0-0
8	♗c4-b3	♘c6-a5?

The drawback of the Accelerated Dragon is that in the opening, Black doesn't have any pawn control in the centre, White's pieces are given a lot of space and Black has to be very careful. Here he isn't at all careful! He moves his knight away from the centre and abandons e5 entirely. How should White take advantage? He could just castle but as in our last game White suspects there ought to be something better. He looks for a combination and finds one!

9	e4-e5!	♘f6-e8

10 ♗b3xf7+!!

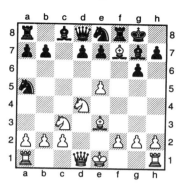

10	...	♔g8xf7

Against either 10...♖f8xf7 or 10...♔g8-h8 White smothers the queen with 11 ♘d4-e6!. However...

11 ♘d4-e6!

...it comes anyway. Black is just zapped right down the middle!

In 1958 the great American Samuel Reshevsky walked into this same variation against a fifteen-year-old Bobby Fischer. To his shame Reshevsky replied 11...d7xe6 and after 12 ♕d1xd8 battled on for another thirty moves. Vasiliev has the grace to go quickly.

11	...	♔f7xe6
12	♕d1-d5+	

The whole centre belongs to White. Black's uncoordinated forces stand helpless in disarray. The king can run...

12	...	♔e6-f5
13	g2-g4+	♔f5xg4
14	♖h1-g1+	♔g4-h3

...but there is nowhere to hide. The white pieces rule the board.

15	♕d5-g2+	♔h3-h4
16	♕g2-g4 mate	

Game 28

...in which control of the centre is the key to a kingside attack.

Posch v Dorrer
Vienna 1958
Four Knights Game

1	e2-e4	e7-e5
2	♘g1-f3	♘b8-c6
3	♘b1-c3	♘g8-f6
4	♗f1-b5	♘c6-d4
5	♘f3xd4	e5xd4
6	e4-e5	d4xc3
7	e5xf6	

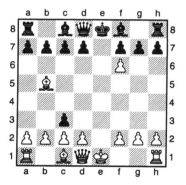

White's plan with 5 ♘f3xd4 and 6 e4-e5 has got him nowhere. Black can now play 7...♕d8xf6 8 d2xc3 ♕f6-e5+ 9 ♕d1-e2 ♕e5xe2+ when a draw looks certain as the material is dead level and the position is completely lifeless.

However, Black wants more; he gets greedy...

| 7 | ... | c3xd2+ |

...he pinches a pawn but loses a lot of time.

| 8 | ♗c1xd2 | ♕d8xf6 |
| 9 | 0-0 | |

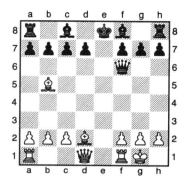

This is a very instructive position. It is not enough to look at the surface and say that White has a lead in development as compensation for the pawn. We must look deeper into the position.

Everything is fine for White! He can seize control of the centre. The e-file is open and his rook is ready for action. His queen has a choice of good squares on the diagonal to h5. When she moves she will leave d1 free for the other rook. The d2-bishop is ready to switch to c3, cutting through the centre and hitting the black queen and kingside.

And what of Black? How can he develop?

One bishop will get employment on e7 blocking the e-file but the other bishop and the rooks have no obvious future. His queen cannot accomplish anything on her own and, out in front of her pawns, she is likely to be a target.

| 9 | ... | ♗f8-e7 |

Black must shut the e-file and castle quickly. 9...♕f6xb2 10 ♖f1-e1+

&f8-e7 11 ♕d1-e2 takes greed a little too far!

10   &d2-c3

When you have a good position good moves flow naturally!

10   ...   ♕f6-g5
11   ♖f1-e1!   0-0

Taking the bishop was no better: 11...♕g5xb5 12 ♕d1-g4! d7-d5 13 ♕g4xg7 ♖h8-f8 14 &c3-f6 &c8-e6 15 ♖e1xe6!.

12   ♖e1-e5   ♕g5-f6
13   &b5-d3!

White could have continued with 13 ♕d1-e2 and then moved the a1-rook to the centre. *But for White the opening is over!* As well as his lead in development he has complete control of the centre and this enables him to switch immediately to a kingside attack.

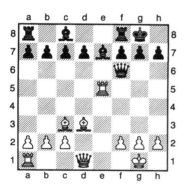

White threatens 14 ♖e5-h5 when he hits h7 head-on and discovers an attack on the black queen.

13   ...   h7-h6

If 13...g7-g6 White has a lovely combination: 14 ♖e5-h5! ♕f6-e6 15 ♖h5xh7! ♔g8xh7 16 ♕d1-h5+ ♔h7-g8 17 ♕h5-h8 mate.

14   ♕d1-g4

With the centre under his full control White finds it easy to switch his pieces to the kingside attack. His queen is headed for e4 when he will have the double threat of mating on h7 and winning the bishop e7.

14   ...   ♕f6-h4

Black stops that threat but walks into a bigger one...

15   ♕g4xg7+!!

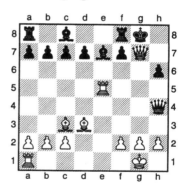

15   ...   ♔g8xg7
16   ♖e5-g5 mate

Look again at the two diagrams on this page. The centre is so often the springboard for a kingside attack. The white bishops raked the diagonals and White's rook and queen powered down the open files. Switching to a mating attack was easy.

Game 29

...in which White achieves his aims but spends too long doing so.

Granat v Yartsev
Israel 1990
Sicilian Defence

1	e2-e4	c7-c5
2	♘g1-f3	e7-e6
3	d2-d4	c5xd4
4	♘f3xd4	♘g8-f6
5	♘b1-c3	♘b8-c6

Black's immediate aim in this, the Four Knights Variation of the Sicilian, is to play ...♝f8-b4. By pinning White's knight he will be threatening his e-pawn. The drawback of Black's set-up is that it leaves a hole on d6, which White is quick to seize upon.

6	♘d4-b5	♝f8-b4

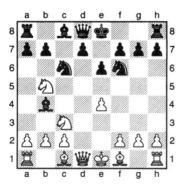

7 ♘b5-d6+?
White has two aims. One is to prevent Black from castling. The other is to reach a position where he has two bishops against two knights.

7 ...   ♚e8-e7!

Black is happy to fall in with White's plans.

8 ♘d6xc8+
White is achieving his aim but he is losing a lot of time. He has just exchanged a knight which had made four moves for a bishop which had made none, and...

8 ...   ♖a8xc8
...he has developed Black's rook for him.

9	♝c1-d2	♝b4xc3
10	♝d2xc3	

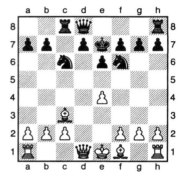

This is just the sort of position White was aiming for. The black king is stuck in the centre, unable to castle. He has two bishops against two knights, which on an open board is generally considered to be an advantage. However...

10 ...   ♘f6xe4
11 ♝c3xg7   ♖h8-g8
...this is just the sort of position Black was anticipating when he gave up his right to castle!

As we have seen in several games it is normally very dangerous to allow the king to be caught in the centre but here the black king is quite happy with his position. He has a pawn shield and there is no way for White to smash open the central files. Furthermore Black has a massive lead in development and this makes it impossible for White to launch an effective attack against the king.

It is Black who has the attack!

12 &g7-d4

Against 12 &g7-c3 or 12 &g7-h6 Black would have hit f2 with a mate threat by 12...♕d8-b6.

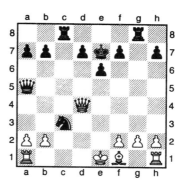

15 b2xc3

Otherwise the knight wreaks havoc with a discovered check.

15 ... ♖c8xc3

16 ♕d4-d2

Otherwise the rook wreaks havoc with a discovered check!

16 ... ♖g8-g5!

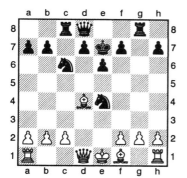

12 ... ♕d8-a5+

Black completes his development, forcing White's reply.

13 c2-c3 ♘c6xd4!

Not only has White lost one of his two bishops but he has lost the only piece he had got in play!

14 ♕d1xd4 ♘e4xc3!!

Black smashes open the position. His pieces are beautifully co-ordinated and they combine for a powerful finish.

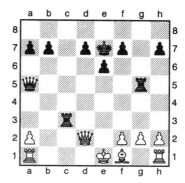

17 Resigns

The threat of 17...♖g5-d5 is absolutely devastating.

Game 30

...in which White triumphs in the 'Battle of the e-file'.

Wolf v Haas
Vienna 1911
Ruy Lopez

1	e2-e4	e7-e5
2	♘g1-f3	♘b8-c6
3	♗f1-b5	♘g8-f6
4	0-0	♘f6xe4
5	d2-d4	♘e4-d6
6	♗b5xc6	b7xc6?

Capturing with the d-pawn is better. After 6...d7xc6 7 d4xe5 ♘d6-f5 8 ♕d1xd8+ ♔e8xd8 Black has a fine game.

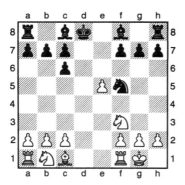

Here White will gain no advantage from catching the black king in the centre. Since the queens have been exchanged the king is in no danger of a direct attack. True, he is in the way of the rooks uniting on e8 and d8 and he will have to move again but it is more important that the rooks and bishops have splendid open lines.

| 7 | d4xe5 | ♘d6-b7? |

Black shunts his knight off into a corner where it blocks the c8-bishop and does not influence the centre. 7...♘d6-f5 is better.

| 8 | ♘b1-c3 | ♗f8-e7 |
| 9 | ♘f3-d4! | |

White has a very good reason for moving this knight a second time.

Black desperately needs to play ...d7-d6 to challenge White's powerful e-pawn and free the line of the c8-bishop. 9 ♘f3-d4 stops this by attacking the c6-pawn.

| 9 | ... | 0-0 |
| 10 | ♗c1-e3 | c6-c5 |

This solves Black's ...d7-d6 problem but he really wanted c5 as a base for his knight.

11	♘d4-f5	d7-d6
12	♘f5xe7+	♕d8xe7
13	♘c3-d5	♕e7-d8

13...♕e7xe5? 14 ♗e3-f4 ♕e5xb2 15 ♖a1-b1 ♕b2xa2 16 ♘d5-e7+ loses a piece.

| 14 | ♕d1-h5? | |

At first sight this looks like a good idea. The queen defends the e-pawn and d1 is left free for a white rook. However, the queen is developed to the side of the board where she has little support for a kingside attack. White does better to play in the centre with 14 e5xd6 c7xd6 15 ♗e3-f4 and then use his queen and rooks on the e- and d-files.

| 14 | ... | ♖f8-e8! |

Good development: the centre is all important. Black realizes the e-file will soon be opened and that he needs to control it.

| 15 | ♗e3-g5!? | |

White gambits a pawn as he proceeds with his risky plan. Again 15 e5xd6 was safer.

15 ... ♖e8xe5

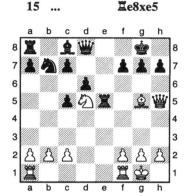

Black has won a pawn. His rook stands proudly centre board. It is on the open e-file, it is forking White's knight and bishop and it seems to be winning a piece.

16 ♖f1-e1!

Just in time White's thoughts return to the centre! The open e-file is the key to the position. Black occupied it but now White is challenging him for control of it.

16 ... f7-f6

Black cannot grab a piece because he is mated immediately if he abandons the e-file, e.g. 16...♖e5xg5 17 ♕h5xg5! ♕d8xg5 18 ♖e1-e8 mate or 16...♖e5xd5 17 ♗g5xd8 ♖d5xh5 18 ♖e1-e8 mate.

Of course 16...♖e5xe1+ 17 ♖a1xe1 just gives the file away.

17 f2-f4 g7-g6??

Black has become over-excited by the chance of winning a piece. He kicks the white queen away to prevent ♖e1-e8+ but ... Oh dear! On g7 his pawn was well placed. Now there is a hole on h6 and the f6-pawn has lost its support. 17...♖e5-e6 was much better.

18 ♕h5-h6

Black's f6-pawn is in trouble and 18...♖e5-e6 19 ♖e1xe6 won't help, so...

18 ... ♖e5xd5

...Black has to surrender the e-file. He wins his piece but...

19 ♗g5xf6!

...f6 collapses and...

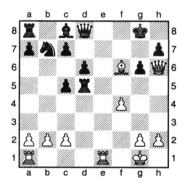

19 ... ♕d8-f8

...the battle of the e-file is over. After 19...♕d8xf6, 20 ♖e1-e8+ mates.

20 ♖e1-e8!!

Yes! White has definitely won the battle of the e-file!

20 ... Resigns

Because 20...♕f8xe8 21 ♕h6-g7 is mate.

Game 31

...in which White opens lines and Black uses them.

J. Rosanes v A. Anderssen
Breslau 1862
King's Gambit

1	e2-e4	e7-e5
2	f2-f4	d7-d5

This is Falkbeer's Counter-Gambit in which Black aims for quick development and complications.

3	e4xd5	e5-e4

On e4 this black pawn is able to make a real nuisance of itself by preventing ♘g1-f3 so now White does best to continue 4 d2-d3. Rosanes has other ideas. He sets out to win the e4-pawn.

4	♗f1-b5+	c7-c6
5	d5xc6	♘b8xc6
6	♘b1-c3	♘g8-f6
7	♕d1-e2	

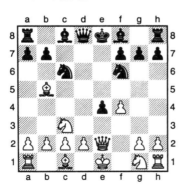

Everything is going as Rosanes planned. He is a pawn up, the black e-pawn is under fire and a king is about

to be caught in the centre. The only problem is...

7	...	♗f8-c5!
8	♘c3xe4	0-0!

...it's his own king which is going to be caught on the file which he himself has generously opened!

What can White do? 9 ♘e4xc5 is no good because of 9...♖f8-e8 and meanwhile Black is simply threatening the same trick: 9...♘f6xe4 10 ♕e2xe4 ♖f8-e8.

9	♗b5xc6	

White doesn't like 9 d2-d3 ♘f6xe4 10 d3xe4 because 10...♘c6-d4 followed by 11...♕d8-a5+ would win his b5-bishop so he solves the problem by chopping off the c6-knight. Unfortunately he also opens the b-file for Black's rook.

9	...	b7xc6

Until Paul Morphy exploded onto the stage, Adolf Anderssen was the top man. He played some of the finest sacrificial games ever seen and is still regarded as one of the game's greatest tactical magicians. Anderssen would have looked at the open files and diagonals and he would have smiled. He would not have bothered counting the pawns!

| 10 | d2-d3 | ♖f8-e8 |
| 11 | ♗c1-d2 | ♘f6xe4! |

Cleverly played. Anderssen can see that White is preparing to castle queenside, after which the open e-file will not be too important, so...

12 d3xe4

...he invites White to block the file with a pawn so that...

| 12 | ... | ♗c8-f5! |

...he can develop his bishop with a threat...

13 e4-e5

...and force White to advance the pawn, thus opening the diagonal from the bishop to c2.

| 13 | ... | ♕d8-b6 |

Threatening both 14...♗c5xg1 and 14...♕b6xb2.

| 14 | 0-0-0 | ♗c5-d4! |

The attack is under way and all roads lead to the white king!

Now Black is threatening mate on b2.

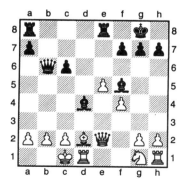

15 c2-c3

This opens the line of Black's f5-bishop even further but 15 b2-b3 allows 15...♕b6-c5 mating.

| 15 | ... | ♖a8-b8 |

Threatening mate on b2 again.

| 16 | b2-b3 | ♖e8-d8!! |

Quiet ... simple ... and deadly!

Anderssen has calculated quite brilliantly. The obvious point is that after 17 c3xd4 ♕b6xd4 he mates on a1. But what is the rook doing on d8, on a file already cluttered with pieces? This deep and subtle point we will understand later.

17 ♘g1-f3

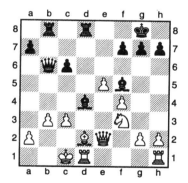

| 17 | ... | ♕b6xb3!! |

Crushing! Anderssen opens lines of his own!

| 18 | a2xb3 | ♖b8xb3 |
| 19 | ♗d2-e1 | ♗d4-e3+! |

Now we see why 16...♖e8-d8 was so clever: 20 ♕e2xe3 ♖b3-b1 is mate because on d8 the rook cuts off the king's escape route.

20 Resigns

Open lines up for yourself ... not your opponent!

Winning in the Opening

Game 32

...in which Black is run over by a steamroller.

V. Sorokin v F. Matveev
Moscow 1995
Giuoco Piano

1	e2-e4	e7-e5
2	♘g1-f3	♘b8-c6
3	♗f1-c4	♗f8-c5
4	c2-c3	♘g8-f6
5	d2-d4	e5xd4
6	c3xd4	♗c5-b6?

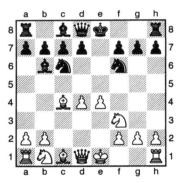

Sorokin's pawns command the board. They attack important squares in the centre and they are mobile, ready to march forward. Black has three pieces in play but he has no pawns giving them shelter or challenging the centre. The pieces simply stand in the path of the advancing steamroller.

7 d4-d5   ♘c6-b8

If 7...♘c6-a5, then 8 ♗c4-d3 and the black knight will soon be threatened with b2-b4. 7...♘c6-e7 might

have been a little bit better ... but not much.

8 e4-e5

The pawns just trundle forward!

8 ...   ♘f6-g8

This time Black didn't have much choice. 8...♘f6-e4 9 d5-d6 c7xd6 10 e5xd6 ♘e4xf2 11 ♕d1-b3 ♘f2xh1 12 ♗c4xf7+ ♔e8-f8 13 ♗c1-g5 wins his queen.

9 0-0   ♘g8-e7

A black knight develops...

10 d5-d6

...so a pawn hits it!

10 ...   ♘e7-g6

10...c7xd6 11 e5xd6 only opens the e-file for White's rook.

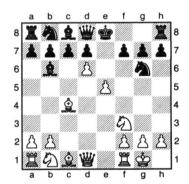

11 ♗c1-g5

The pawns have crushed everything in their path. Now the pieces finish the job.

11	...	f7-f6
12	e5xf6	g7xf6
13	♖f1-e1+	♔e8-f8
14	♗g5-h6 mate	

Pieces cannot stand alone in the face of a pawn onslaught. Black paid the penalty for not getting a pawn in the centre.

Game 33

...in which White learns that half a point is better than none.

L. Lavrovsky v B. Ryzhenko
St Petersburg 1996
Ruy Lopez

1	e2-e4	e7-e5
2	♘g1-f3	♘b8-c6
3	♗f1-b5	a7-a6
4	♗b5xc6	d7xc6
5	0-0	♗c8-g4
6	h2-h3	h7-h5!

This is all opening theory. Now after 7 h3xg4 h5xg4 8 ♘f3xe5 ♕d8-h4 the game would come to an unhappy end for the white king!

7 c2-c3
As he can't take the bishop White plans to push forward in the centre with 8 d2-d4. However...
7 ... ♕d8-d3!
Ryzhenko spots a hole, leaps in and stops dead both Lavrovsky's plan and his development.
8 h3xg4 h5xg4
Usually rooks develop towards the centre but without moving the h8-rook has found a nice open file!
9 ♘f3xe5 ♗f8-d6!
Now after 10 ♘e5xd3 ♗d6-h2+ 11 ♔g1-h1 ♗h2-g3+ Black would force a draw by perpetual check. A draw? Lavrovsky is a piece up ... greedily he wants more.
10 ♘e5xg4? ♘g8-f6
11 ♘g4xf6+ g7xf6
Lavrovsky is now wishing he had taken the draw. He can now see what

he should have seen three moves ago. He is behind in development and Black has the attack. He can't play d2-d4 and he can't develop any of his queenside pieces in a useful direction. Now he has had to open the g-file and Ryzhenko's rooks will soon be united at battle stations.
12 g2-g3
12 ♕d1-f3 loses spectacularly to 12...♖h8-h1+!, and 12 f2-f3 ♗d6-c5+ isn't much better.

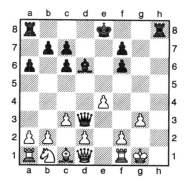

12	...	♗d6xg3
13	f2-f3	

13 f2xg3 ♕d3xg3 is mate straight away.

13 ... 0-0-0!
Reinforcements are needed! The g-file beckons the d8-rook.
14 ♖f1-f2
Otherwise after 14...♖d8-g8 Black mates by moving the bishop.

14	...	♗g3xf2+
15	♔g1xf2	♖h8-h2+
16	♔f2-g3	♖d8-g8+!!
17	♔g3xh2	♕d3-d6+
18	♔h2-h1	♕d6-g3
19	**Resigns**	

Half a point is better than none!

Game 34

...in which White digs the holes and Black fills them in.

P. Esepin v T. Plisitskaya
Moscow 1996
Alekhine's Defence

1	e2-e4	♘g8-f6
2	♘b1-c3	d7-d5
3	e4xd5	♘f6xd5
4	♘g1-e2	♘b8-c6
5	g2-g3	

With 4 ♘g1-e2 White blocked the lines of his queen and bishop.

Now he should have untangled himself by 5 ♘c3xd5 ♕d8xd5 6 ♘e2-c3. Instead he continues with his slow development, playing a pawn move which leaves holes on f3 and h3.

| 5 | ... | ♗c8-g4 |

By aggressive development Black is already beginning to seize the initiative. She is pinning the white knight and targeting the f3-hole.

| 6 | ♗f1-g2 | ♘c6-d4! |

Black can be forgiven for moving her knight a second time. Her pieces are already better placed and by taking up a powerful central position her knight hits f3 and adds to the pin on White's e2-knight. Now 7...♘d5xc3 winning a piece is threatened.

| 7 | ♗g2xd5?? | |

Ugh! Really dreadful! The last thing you want to do with a fianchettoed bishop is to swap it for a knight and leave the holes unprotected. Plisitskaya has a stunning reply ready!

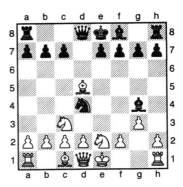

| 7 | ... | ♕d8xd5!! |

Now White has no control at all over either f3 or h3 and is mated if he takes the queen: 8 ♘c3xd5 ♘d4-f3+ 9 ♔e1-f1 ♗g4-h3 mate. A very pretty finish!

| 8 | 0-0 | |

The king leaps from one grave to another. The holes are filled in around him just the same.

8	...	♘d4-f3+
9	♔g1-h1	♘f3-g5+
10	♘c3xd5	♗g4-f3+
11	♔h1-g1	♘g5-h3 mate

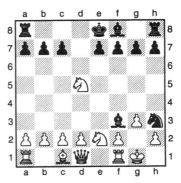

Dead and buried!

Basic Principles: The Tests

OK. We've explained the principles, you've learned the commandments and you have seen some glorious games warning you of the painful death which awaits the player who breaks them!

Now it's your turn again.

On the following pages are twenty-eight test positions.

You should begin by studying carefully each diagram to try to understand what is happening in the position (the letter *W* or *B* will tell you whose turn it is to move).

Look to see if either side has a lead in development, better-placed pieces or greater control of the centre.

Look to see if either player has such an advantage he can play immediately for the attack.

Look to see which pieces remain to be developed and consider where they should go.

Then look at the three candidate moves 'a', 'b' and 'c' given underneath the diagram and use your knowledge of the basic principles to judge them. You will not necessarily be looking for a winning move! You will simply be considering whether each of the three moves is good or bad. (You will find the answers on the page opposite the diagrams.)

And be warned! Whilst you are busy thinking about the basic principles of development and the centre, *keep your eyes open!* Remember the tactical themes. There will be tactical traps for you to find or fall into just as there were in our Tactics Test ... and just as there will be in your own games!

1. *B*

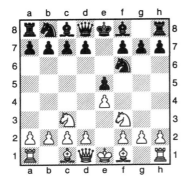

a) ...♘b8-c6
b) ...♗f8-d6
c) ...♕d8-e7

3. *W*

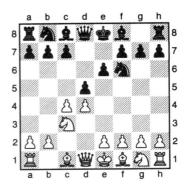

a) ♕d1-a4+
b) ♘g1-f3
c) f2-f4

2. *W*

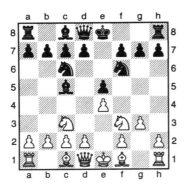

a) ♗f1-c4
b) ♘f3-g5
c) ♗f1-g2

4. *B*

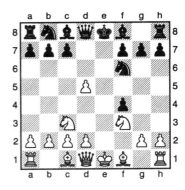

a) ...♗f8-c5
b) ...♕d8-e7+
c) ...♘f6xd5

1. Black's e-pawn is attacked. How should he save it?

a) 1...♘b8-c6 is best. It is an excellent developing move and it also defends the e-pawn.

b) After 1...♗f8-d6 the bishop is badly placed. It has nothing to do on its new diagonal as it is blocked by the pawns on e5 and c7. It is also getting in the way of its own d-pawn, which in turn is blocking in the c8-bishop and the black queen.

c) 1...♕d8-e7 is also a poor move as it blocks the diagonal of the f8-bishop.

2.

a) 1 ♗f1-c4 would be the best developing move if White had not already played the pawn move g2-g3. Now the bishop is needed on the kingside to guard the holes on f3 and h3.

b) 1 ♘f3-g5 unnecessarily moves a piece a second time and begins an attack on f7 when White is behind in development and has no pieces ready to support the knight.

c) 1 ♗f1-g2 is a good move, developing a piece and controlling f3 and h3.

3.

a) 1 ♕d1-a4+ does not achieve anything because Black has several good ways of getting out of check. The queen is the most powerful piece. She does not belong on the edge of the board and she should not be developed early. White should wait until he knows where she might be useful before committing her.

b) 1 ♘g1-f3 is a good developing move. It supports the d4-pawn, it attacks the centre and it helps clear the way for castling.

c) 1 f2-f4 is an unnecessary pawn move which wastes time and gets in the way by blocking the path of the c1-bishop.

4.

a) 1...♗f8-c5 puts the bishop on a splendid diagonal but it is still a bad move because White will simply reply 2 d2-d4 and gain time driving the bishop away.

b) 1...♕d8-e7+ is bad because it blocks the line of the f8-bishop. Furthermore, White will play 2 ♗f1-e2 and 3 0-0 and hope to catch Black's king on the open e-file.

c) 1...♘f6xd5 is a good move. Although the knight moves a second time it captures a pawn, it defends the f4-pawn and it occupies a fine central square.

5. *W*

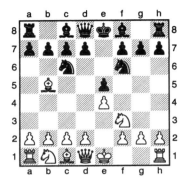

a) ♘f3-g5
b) ♗b5xc6
c) d2-d4

7. *W*

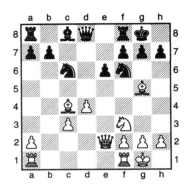

a) ♖a1-e1
b) ♗c4-b5
c) ♖f1-e1

6. *B*

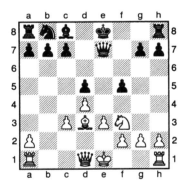

a) ...0-0
b) ...♕e7-a3
c) ...h7-h6

8. *W*

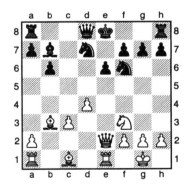

a) ♗c1-e3
b) ♗c1-g5
c) ♗c1-a3

5.

a) 1 ♘f3-g5 is a poor move. It moves the knight unnecessarily for a second time and without support the knight poses no threat to f7.

b) 1 ♗b5xc6 is also poor. It unnecessarily exchanges the bishop and after 1...d7xc6 it opens the diagonal for Black's c8-bishop. Notice that 2 ♘f3xe5 ♕d8-d4 is good for Black.

c) 1 d2-d4 is a good move. It challenges the centre and opens the lines for White's queen and c1-bishop.

6.

a) 1...0-0 is an excellent move, tucking the king away safely in the corner and bringing the rook into play. Black may later play ...♖f8-e8 or ...f5-f4 to give more power to the rook.

b) 1...♕e7-a3 is a poor move. Black has no right to begin an attack with only his queen in play. 2 ♕d1-c2 is a simple reply for White, developing the queen, guarding c3 and attacking f5. Black's queen is nicely developed on e7 on the half-open file: he should leave her there.

c) 1...h7-h6 is awful! It does nothing and it leaves a hole on g6.

7. White has everything in play apart from the rooks. Rooks need open files. e1 is a good square for a rook as it supports the queen on the e-file. d1 is a good square as it prepares to open lines with d4-d5. b1 is a good square as it puts pressure on Black's b-pawn. So...

a) 1 ♖a1-e1 is poor because it leaves the f1-rook without a square.

b) 1 ♗c4-b5 unnecessarily moves the well-placed bishop a second time.

c) 1 ♖f1-e1 is a good developing move.

8. The question is where to put the bishop.

a) e3 is a poor home as the bishop blocks its own pieces on the e-file and is blocked itself by the f2- and d4-pawns.

b) g5, where it will pin the knight, is a fine developing square.

c) a3 is best because it attacks f8, stops Black from castling, traps his king in the centre and threatens the murderous 2 ♗b3xe6!. If Black defends with 1...♘d7-f8 White can build up a powerful attack with 2 ♖a1-d1 and 3 d4-d5, smashing open the lines to the black king.

(Note that White may win a pawn with 1 ♗b3xe6 if he prefers, although that gives Black time to play 1...0-0 and tuck his king safely away.)

9. *B*

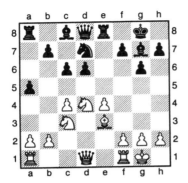

a) ...♕d8-h4
b) ...♘d7-c5
c) ...♗g7xd4

11. *W*

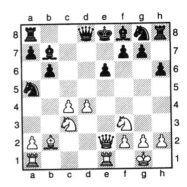

a) ♖a1-b1
b) ♖a1-d1
c) d4-d5

10. *W*

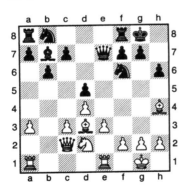

a) e3-e4
b) ♘d2-f3
c) ♗d3-h7+

12. *B*

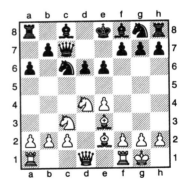

a) ...♘g8-e7
b) ...♘g8-f6
c) ...g7-g6

9.

a) 1...♕d8-h4 develops the queen, but to the side of the board and it is not easy for Black's other pieces to join in a kingside attack.

b) 1...♘d7-c5 is a good move. The knight takes up a central post attacking e4 and it clears the diagonal for the c8-bishop.

c) 1...♗g7xd4 is dreadful because the bishop is needed to defend the holes, the squares f6 and h6, around his king. It is also strongly placed where it is on g7, attacking the centre, so why exchange it?

10. All White's pieces are nicely co-ordinated to support the advance of his e-pawn.

a) 1 e3-e4 is the natural move, threatening 2 e4-e5 winning a piece and 2 e4xd5 opening the e-file.

b) 1 ♘d2-f3 seems to put the knight on a better square but it does not fit in with White's plan and spoils his co-ordination.

c) 1 ♗d3-h7+ looks flashy since the black knight is pinned and the bishop cannot be captured. However, after 1...♔g8-h8 White has achieved nothing and his bishop, which looks

rather silly on h7, will always be in danger.

11.

a) 1 ♖a1-b1 puts the rook on a half-open file but it is blocked by the bishop and it isn't clear what the rook will be able to do.

b) 1 ♖a1-d1 puts the rook on a much better square, supporting White's centre and eyeing up the black queen.

c) 1 d4-d5 is an excellent move, which will smash open the central files so that White's better-developed pieces can get at the black king.

12.

a) 1...♘g8-e7? blocks the f8-bishop and clutters Black's position up so much that White can win immediately. After 2 ♘d4-b5! a6xb5 3 ♘c3xb5 all moves by the black queen are met by 4 ♘b5xd6+ winning material.

b) 1...♘g8-f6 puts the knight on its best square, attacking the centre.

c) 1...g7-g6 intends to fianchetto the f8-bishop but the bishop is needed to defend the d6-pawn and should go to e7. After 1...g7-g6 Black has holes on f6 and h6 and this gives his bishop too much work to do.

13. *B*

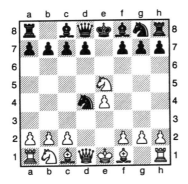

a) ...c7-c5
b) ...♗f8-c5
c) ...f7-f6

15. *W*

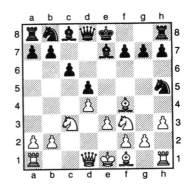

a) ♗f4-h2
b) ♗f4-g3
c) ♗f4xb8

14. *W*

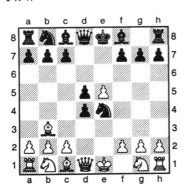

a) ♘g1-f3
b) a2-a3
c) ♕d1xd4

16. *W*

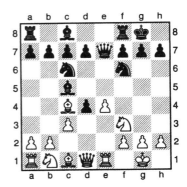

a) ♕d1-b3
b) e4-e5
c) c3xd4

13.

a) 1...c7-c5 defends the knight but is a poor move because it blocks the diagonal of the f8-bishop and leaves holes on d5 and d6.

b) 1...♗f8-c5? is a blunder. It loses a pawn to the familiar 2 ♘e5xf7 ♔e8xf7 3 ♕d1-h5+ and 4 ♕h5xc5.

c) 1...f7-f6? is a bad move which can be punished by 2 ♕d1-h5+ g7-g6 3 ♘e5xg6 ♘d4xc2+ 4 ♔e1-d1 ♘c2xa1 5 ♘g6-e5+ ♔e8-e7 6 ♕h5-f7+ ♔e7-d6 7 ♘e5-c4+ ♔d6-c5 8 ♕f7-d5+ ♔c5-b4 9 ♕d5-a5 mate.

(Black should play either 1...♘d4-c6 or 1...♘d4-e6)

14.

a) 1 ♘g1-f3 is a sensible developing move which defends the e-pawn and attacks the black pawn on d4.

b) White is in no danger after 1...♗f8-b4+ so 1 a2-a3 is a pointless pawn move.

c) Don't forget the tactics! The move 1 ♕d1xd4? is a mistake. Black replies 1...♗f8-c5 2 ♕d4xd5 ♕d8xd5 3 ♗b3xd5 ♘e4xf2 and ends up winning a rook.

15. The black knight is on the edge of the board and White doesn't want

to allow it to chop off his nice f4-bishop. But where should the bishop go?

a) 1 ♗f4-h2 keeps the bishop on its good diagonal and leaves the black knight loose on h5. A sensible move!

b) 1 ♗f4-g3 is just silly! Black can still exchange knight for bishop and after 1...♘h5xg3 2 f2xg3 White's pawn position is wrecked and he has weaknesses on e4, e3 and g3.

c) 1 ♗f4xb8 is poor because it exchanges a well-placed bishop for a knight which has not yet moved.

16.

a) The move 1 ♕d1-b3 doesn't actually threaten either f7 or b7. Black answers it easily with 1...♘c6-a5 and then 2...♘a5xc4.

b) 1 e4-e5 looks dangerous but invites 1...♘f6-g4 which attacks f2, h2, and e5. Now after 2 c3xd4 ♘c6xd4! 3 ♘f3xd4 Black takes immediate advantage of the fact that the white king has been abandoned by his pieces. 3...♕e7-h4 4 ♘d4-f3 ♕h4xf2+ 5 ♔g1-h1 ♕f2-g1+! 6 ♘f3xg1 (or 6 ♖e1xg1) 6...♘g4-f2 is mate.

c) 1 c3xd4 regains the pawn, attacks the black bishop and sets up a magnificent centre.

17. B

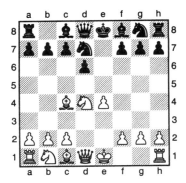

a) ...♗f8-e7
b) ...♘g8-f6
c) ...c7-c5

19. W

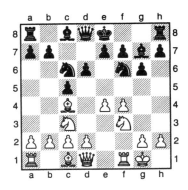

a) e4-e5
b) d2-d4
c) d2-d3

18. B

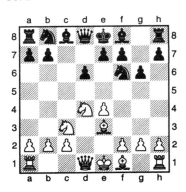

a) ...♗f8-g7
b) ...♘f6-g4
c) ...e7-e5

20. B

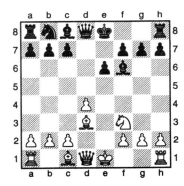

a) ...0-0
b) ...h7-h6
c) ...♗f6xd4

17.
a) Beware the tactics! 1...♝f8-e7 seems a reasonable developing move but is actually a blunder because it leaves the black royal family without any air. After 2 ♝c4xf7+! ♚e8xf7 3 ♞d4-e6! Black can choose between 3...♚f7xe6 4 ♕d1-d5+ ♚e6-f6 5 ♕d5-f5 mate and 3...♕d8-e8 when 4 ♞e6xc7 followed by 5 ♕d1-d5+ and 6 ♞c7-e6 still costs Black his queen.
b) 1...♞g8-f6 is a sound developing move.
c) 1...c7-c5 leaves a hole on d5 and a weak pawn on d6 which White can immediately attack with 2 ♞d4-f5.

18.
a) 1...♝f8-g7 is a sensible developing move.
b) 1...♞f6-g4? is a blunder allowing 2 ♝f1-b5+ when 2...♝c8-d7 and 2...♞b8-d7 both lose a piece to 3 ♕d1xg4, and 2...♞b8-c6 3 ♞d4xc6 b7xc6 4 ♝b5xc6+ loses the exchange and a pawn.
c) 1...e7-e5 drives the white knight out of the centre but the pawn leaves behind holes on d5 and f6 and a weak pawn on d6. Furthermore on e5 the pawn will block the f8-bishop when it develops to g7.

19.
a) 1 e4-e5 loses a pawn since after 1...d6xe5 2 f4xe5 ♞c6xe5! 3 ♞f3xe5 ♕d8-d4+ the white knight is loose.
b) 1 d2-d4 also loses material: 1...c5xd4 2 ♞f3xd4 ♕d8-b6! 3 ♝c1-e3 ♞f6-g4 leaves the d4-knight in trouble.
c) 1 d2-d3 defending the e-pawn and opening the line of the c1-bishop is natural and good.

20.
a) 1...0-0 is sensible early castling, putting the king out of harm's way and bringing the rook towards the centre.
b) 1...h7-h6 is an unnecessary pawn move. White couldn't put a piece on g5 even if he wanted to.
c) Re-read the section on tactical themes if you wanted to pinch the pawn! 1...♝f6xd4? 2 ♞f3xd4 ♕d8xd4? 3 ♝d3-b5+ has been seen before!

21. *B*

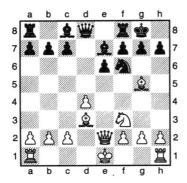

a) ...b7-b6
b) ...g7-g6
c) ...c7-c5

23. *B*

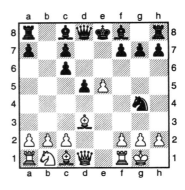

a) ...♗f8-c5
b) ...♘g4xe5
c) ...♗c8-e6

22. *B*

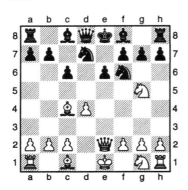

a) ...h7-h6
b) ...♕d8-e7
c) ...♘d7-b6

24. *B*

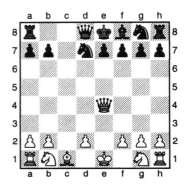

a) ...b7-b6
b) ...♖a8-c8
c) ...♘d7-c5

21.

a) 1...b7-b6? leaves the rook loose in the corner. Normally this wouldn't be a problem as Black would play 2...♗c8-b7 and have a satisfactory position, but here it is a blunder: 2 ♗g5xf6 ♗e7xf6 3 ♕e2-e4 'forks' the rook and mate on h7.

b) 1...g7-g6 is a pointless pawn move which leaves holes on f6 and h6.

c) 1...c7-c5 challenging the centre is a sound move.

22. White has an attack on the target square f7 and his queen and bishop are lined up in support.

a) 1...h7-h6? only drives the knight where it wants to go and loses immediately: 2 ♘g5xf7! (forking queen and rook) 2...♔e8xf7 3 ♕e2xe6+ ♔f7-g6 4 ♗c4-d3+ ♔g6-h5 5 ♕e6-h3 mate.

b) 1...♕d8-e7 prevents the knight sacrifice but the queen is poorly placed on e7 where she blocks the f8-bishop.

c) 1...♘d7-b6 solves the problem of the mate threat and gains time by attacking White's bishop.

23.

a) 1...♗f8-c5 is an excellent aggressive developing move. It does not actually threaten anything but by attacking f2 it prevents White from supporting his e-pawn by either 2 ♖f1-e1 or 2 f2-f4.

b) 1...♘g4xe5? is a blunder which loses the knight to the familiar pin on the e-file: 2 ♖f1-e1 ♗f8-d6 3 f2-f4.

c) 1...♗c8-e6 is a good developing move but 1...♗f8-c5 is better because it restricts White's replies and it prepares for rapid castling.

24.

a) It would be very risky for White to waste time with ♕e4xb7 so it is not necessary for Black to save his pawn and waste a move of his own with 1...b7-b6.

b) 1...♖a8-c8 is a splendid developing move, putting the rook on an open file and attacking the white bishop.

c) Although it moves the knight a second time, 1...♘d7-c5 is best because it attacks both the white queen and the hole on d3. The game might continue with 2 ♕e4-c4 ♘c5-d3+ 3 ♔e1-e2 ♖a8-c8 4 ♕c4xd3 ♕d8xd3+ 5 ♔e2xd3 ♖c8xc1 when it is hard to imagine how White is ever going to evict the rook from his first rank and develop any of his pieces!

25. *B*

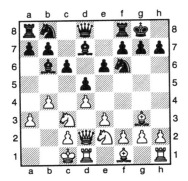

a) ...a7-a5
b) ...♘f6-h5
c) ...♘b8-a6

27. *B*

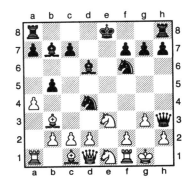

a) ...h7-h5
b) ...♘d4xb3
c) ...0-0

26. *W*

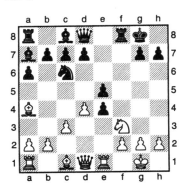

a) ♖e1xe4
b) ♘f3xe5
c) ♗c1-g5

28. *W*

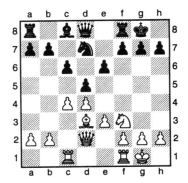

a) ♕d2-c2
b) c4xd5
c) e3-e4

25. White has castled but not into safety as the pawns which should be sheltering him have gone for a walk. Black's middlegame plan will be to launch a queenside attack.

a) 1...a7-a5 is an excellent line-opening pawn move which will help the rook develop directly into the attack on the white king.

b) 1...♘f6-h5 places the knight on the edge of the wrong side of the board where it will not co-ordinate with Black's plans and other pieces. If he follows up with 2...♘h5xg3 3 h2xg3 he has wasted two moves opening the h-file for White's rook to use.

c) 1...♘b8-a6 develops the knight but blocks the a-pawn.

26.

a) 1 ♖e1xe4 invites Black to play 1...d7-d5 driving the rook away and opening the line for the c8-bishop.

b) 1 ♘f3xe5 allows 1...♘c6xe5 2 d4xe5, which opens the diagonal for the a7-bishop to join in a fierce attack on f2.

c) 1 ♗c1-g5 develops a piece and gains time by attacking the queen. Now, after 1...♕d8-e8 White can play 2 ♖e1xe4 and Black can't reply 2...d7-d5 due to 3 ♖e4xe5 ♘c6xe5 4 ♗a4xe8.

27. Black has a lead in development and command of the centre.

a) Attack! 1...h7-h5 followed by 2...h5-h4 will force open the h-file and lead to a mating attack by queen and rook.

b) 1...♘d4xb3 2 c2xb3 would leave White with a weak pawn on b3 and a hole on d3 ... two benefits! But why exchange such a beautifully centralized knight?

c) 1...0-0 would normally be an excellent move but the king is in absolutely no danger in the centre and the rook is needed on the h-file.

28.

a) 1 ♕d2-c2 is not bad but it moves a piece a second time and does not help White use his advantage in development and space to seize the initiative. Black can answer 1...♘d7-f6.

b) 1 c4xd5 is a reasonable plan. After 1...e6xd5 White can start an attack on the queenside with b2-b4 and b4-b5.

c) 1 e3-e4 seizes the initiative and gains more space. Black either has to allow 2 e4-e5 or play 1...d5xe4 giving White a powerful, space-controlling pawn centre and open lines for his pieces.

Answers to Test Questions (on pages 32-40)

Read the answers to the test positions carefully! Most of the positions contained a lot of ideas so there is much more to learn than just finding out whether you were correct.

1. 1 ♕g4xg6+!! h7xg6 2 ♗d3xg6 mate. (Of course 1 ♗d3xg6+ is just as good ... but it's always a nice feeling to sacrifice the queen!)

2. The black king has to defend d8 and f7, so: 1 ♗c4xf7+ ♔e8xf7 2 ♕d1xd8 wins the queen.

3. The e-file! 1 ♖f1-e1 pins the knight and if a black pawn defends, 2 d2-d3 will win the piece.

4. The white knight may look dangerous but it is also loose. 1...♕d8-a5+ wins the knight.

5. Black has something much better! 1...♘e5-d3 mate.

6. Noah's Ark! 1 c4-c5 ♗b6-a5 2 b2-b4 traps the bishop.

7. Yes! 1 ♕d1-h5+ ♔e8-e7 2 ♕h5-f7+ ♔e7-d6 3 ♘e5-c4 mate.

8. 1 ♗d3xe4! wins a piece. Black cannot recapture as 1...♕d5xe4 2 ♖f1-e1 wins the queen. Notice that 1 ♖f1-e1 is not as good since Black plays

1...f7-f5 and there is no white pawn ready to attack the knight.

9. The h5-bishop is trapped in a Noah's Ark but White must get his move-order correct. 1 f2-f4 ♘e5-c6 (or 1...♘e5-g6 2 g2-g4) 2 g2-g4 ♗h5-g6 3 f4-f5 wins the bishop *but* if White plays his combination the other way round then he loses material himself: 1 g2-g4 ♘e5-f3 forking queen and rook.

10. f2 and the e-file are the keys to open the door. 1...♘e4xf2 2 ♔e1xf2 ♕e7xe3+ 3 ♔f2-g2 ♕e3-f2 mate. Of course White can avoid mate if he doesn't play 2 ♔e1xf2 but then he has queen, rook and e-pawn all *en prise*.

11. ...b7-b6 leaves the a8-rook loose. 1 ♕e2-e4 hits the rook and also threatens mate on h7. Black can't defend against both threats.

12. No! Black has won a pawn after 1 ♘f3xd4 ♕d8xd4 but then it is White's turn to do the winning: 2 ♗d3xh7+ ♔g8xh7 3 ♕d1xd4.

13. White's king is rudely awoken by 1...♕d8-b6 knocking on his front door. He can't defend f2 and knight moves to b3, c3, f3 or g3 are all answered by 2...♗c5xf2+ and 3...♕b6-e3 mate.

Notice that 1...♗c5xf2+ 2 ♔e1xf2 ♕d8-b6+ (or 2...♕d8-h4+) gets nowhere because Black does not have any more pieces in play to follow up the attack.

14. 1 ♕d1-d5! threatens mate on f7. 1...♘g8-h6 2 ♗c1xh6 simply loses a piece so Black must move his other knight. Then 2 ♕d5xf7+ follows and the black king is on the run. Again 1 ♗c4xf7+ is no good: 1...♔e8xf7 2 ♕d1-d5+ ♔f7-f8 and Black is safe.

15. 1...c7-c5 2 ♘d4-e2 c5-c4 and we have Noah's familiar Ark!

16. 1...♘c6xd4 2 ♘f3xd4 ♕d8xd4!! 3 ♕d1xd4 and the now the white queen is loose to what is known as the family fork: 3...♘b4xc2+. Black regains his queen and pockets two pawns.

17. 1 ♘g5xf7!! threatens to win a rook, so: 1...♔e8xf7 2 ♗d3-g6+! ♔f7xg6 3 ♕d1xd4 wins the queen for two pieces.

18. Again yes! 1 ♕b3-a4+ and 1 ♕b3-b5+ are both simply answered by 1...♘b8-c6 defending the loose bishop. Therefore: 1 ♗f4xb8 ♖a8xb8 and now a queen check wins the bishop.

19. He should play 1 ♕e2xe4+!. If Black grabs the queen he is mated on f7: 1...♘f6xe4 2 ♗c4xf7 mate. If he doesn't take the queen he loses everything on the e-file: 1...♘d7-e5 2 ♕e4xe5+ ♗c8-e6 3 ♗c4xe6, etc.

20. f2 is the weak point and the knight on g5 is loose, so: 1...♗c5xf2+ 2 ♔e1xf2 ♘f6-g4+ 3 ♔f2-e1 ♕d8xg5. Black has regained his piece, won a pawn, stopped White from castling and he threatens 4...♘g4-e3.

21. It's f7 again! White threatens mate with 1 ♕d1-h5. Then 1...g7-g6 2 ♕h5-d5 'forks' the f7 mate and the rook in the corner.

22. The black king cannot move, so when White plays 1 ♘d4-f5 he threatens both mate on e7 and 2 ♕d1xd5. If 1...♕d5-c5 then 2 ♕d1-d8 mate.

23. Head on! 1 ♗c4xf7+ ♔e8xf7 2 ♘f3xe5+ ♔f7-e8 3 ♕d1xd4 wins a pawn and opens up the black king. Neither 1 ♘f3xe5 nor 1 ♘f3-g5 is as good because Black can defend with 1...♘d4-e6.

24. 1...♕f5xf2+ and White cannot capture because 2 ♔g1xf2 ♗f8-c5 is mate. After 2 ♔g1-h1 ♕f2xe1+ White is a rook down and he has to give up even more pieces to avoid mate.

25. Yes it does work because after 1...♔e8xf7 2 ♘f3-e5+ White wins the piece back on g4. No, there isn't anything better as the flashy 1 ♘f3-e5 is met not by 1...♗g4xd1 2 ♗c4xf7 mate, nor by 1...♗g4-h5 2 ♕d1xh5!, but by 1...♗g4-e6 which saves the bishop and blocks the attack on f7.

26. No! White can make use of the fact that the black bishop on b7 is loose: 1 ♘e5-f7! ♔e8xf7 2 d5xe6+ ♔f7xe6

3 ♗g2xb7 ♘b8-d7 4 ♗b7xa8 ♕d8xa8
5 0-0. White has won the exchange
and Black's king is going for a walk!

27. 1 ♘e5-g6! threatens a great
forking check on e7: 1...♕d5-b7 2
♕f5-d5! ♘b8-c6 3 ♕d5xc6!.

28. 1...♘f6xe4 simply wins a piece
since 2 ♗g5xd8 ♗d6-b4+ 3 ♔e1-e2
♖f8xf2+ 4 ♔e2-e3 ♗b4-c5+ 5 ♔e3xe4
♗c8-f5+ 6 ♔e4xe5 ♘b8-d7 is mate.

29. After 1 e4-e5! d6xe5 2 ♗g2xc6
b7xc6 3 ♘c3-d5! Black can resign
since both 4 ♘d5xe7 mate and 4
♕d2xa5 are threatened. Black can
only avoid this by giving up the knight
on f6 or by not recapturing on c6.

30. Yes, but not by the obvious
methods! 1...f7-f5 2 f2-f3 ♕d8-h4+ 3
♗f4-g3 is no good and 1...♕d8-e7 2
♘d4-f5 ♕e7-e6 3 ♘f5xg7+ is even
worse. Black saves himself by turning
the tables and using the e-file against
White. Black plays 1...0-0!. Now if 2
♕e2xe4 ♖f8-e8, Black wins!

31. Knights were made for forking!
1...♗h4xf2+ wins because 2 ♔e1xf2
♘e5-g4+ and 2 ♕e3xf2 ♘e5xd3+
both fork king and queen.

32. 1 ♗b3-f7+ ♔e8xf7 2 e5-e6+
♗c8xe6 3 ♕h5xa5 wins. If Black simply escapes the bishop check by moving his king to f8 or d8 then White
plays 2 ♗f7xg6 and Black will lose
his rook if he recaptures.

33. Black continues 1...♘f6xd5 because after 2 c4xd5 ♗b4xc3+ 3 b2xc3
the white queen is loose and lost:
3...♕e4xa4.

34. The obvious 1...♗b6xf2+ does
not work because of 2 ♗h4xf2 so it is
Legall time: 1...♘f6xe4 2 ♗h4xd8
♗b6xf2+ 3 ♔e1-e2 ♗c8-g4+ 4 ♔e2-
d3 ♘c6-e5+ 5 ♔d3xe4 f7-f5+ 6 ♔e4-
f4 ♘e5-g6 mate. White does best to
play 2 ♕d1-h5, when he is just a pawn
down.

35. 1 ♘e5xf7 forks the queen and
rook so 1...♔e8xf7 is forced. Now 2
♕b3xe6+ ♔f7-f8 gets nowhere. White
wins by playing 2 ♗d3-g6+! h7xg6 3
♕b3xe6+ ♔f7-f8 4 ♘f4xg6 mate. If
Black doesn't play 2...h7xg6 he loses
his queen: 2...♔f7-f8 3 ♘f4xe6+.

36. A final reminder for you of the
importance of f7 and the h-file diagonal: 1 ♖f1xf5 g6xf5 2 ♕d1xh5+
♖h7xh5 3 ♗c4-f7 mate.

Index of Players

Numbers refer to pages.

Index of Openings

Numbers refer to pages.